Also by Joseph D. Reich

If I Told You To Jump Off The Brooklyn Bridge (Flutter Press)
A Different Sort Of Distance (Skive Magazine Press)
Pain Diary: Working Methadone & The Life & Times Of The Man Sawed In Half (Brick Road Poetry Press)
Drugstore Sushi (Thunderclap Press)
The Derivation Of Cowboys & Indians (Fomite Press)
The Housing Market: a comfortable place to jump off the end of the world (Fomite Press)
The Hole That Runs Through Utopia (Fomite Press)
Connecting The Dots To Shangrila: A Postmodern Cultural Hx Of America (Fomite Press)
Taking The Fifth And Running With It: a psychological guide for the hard of hearing and blind (Broadstone Books)
The Rituals Of Mummification (Sagging Meniscus Press)
Magritte's Missing Murals: Insomniac Episodes (Sagging Meniscus Press)
The Hospitality Business (Valeviel Press)
How To Order Chinese During A Hostage Crisis: Dialects, Existential Essays, A Play, And Other Poems (Hog Press)
The American Book Of The Dead (Xi Draconis Books)
American Existentialism (Tuba Press)
From Premonition To Prophecy (Delinkwent Scholar Press)
An Eccentric Urban Guide to Surviving (Analog Submission Press)
Statutes Of David (Pen & Anvil Press)
A Town With An Ice Cream Stand, Insane Asylum, Pig Farm, Clocktower & Country Club (Musehick Press)

A Case Study Of Werewolves

Joseph D. Reich

Copyright 2019 © Joseph D. Reich
All rights reserved. No part of this book may be reproduced in any form or by any means without the prior written consent of the publisher, except in the case of brief quotations used in reviews and certain other noncommercial uses permitted by copyright law.
ISBN-13: 978-1-944388-86-7
Library of Congress Control Number: 2018967925
Fomite
58 Peru Street
Burlington, VT 05401
www.fomitepress.com

Contents

How I Been Getting By	1
On The Domestic Front	2
He Be Jesus	3
Soulmates	4
Melancholia	5
Rosebud And The Smallprint Below	6
The Long And Short Term Goals Of The Pickpocket And Pot Of Gold At The End Of The Rainbow	7
Plainclothesman	8
American Kulture	10
Truffles & Ticking Bombs	11
The Hx Of Cinema In America	12
A Distorted Different Sort Of American Dream	13
The (not so) Secret Formula	16
Amerika The Beautiful	17
How To Swim Safely Around A Nuclear Missile After A Test Launch With A Couple Cute Rich Girls From The Island You're Trying To Get With Or At Least Store Safe & Secure In Your Jerk-Off Folklore	18
Those Treasures Found At The Bottom Of A Box of Cereal	19
A Case Study Of Werewolves	20
Bowling For Dollars	21
Blueprint For A Life Of Leisure	22
The Life & Times Of Goofus & Gallant	23
A Missing Stage Of Evolution	24
The Anatomical Structure Of Flight	25
Briefcases, Mulch & Garage Door Openers	26
Life Insurance	28
Wichita, KS	29
Days Of Polaroids & Arlo Guthrie	30
Before & After (The Captain America Action/Adventure Existential Version)	31
Like Hot Air Balloons Taking Off In Tornadoes	33
Civilization 101 – 101	34
Wasted	35
Lullabies (or the brothers from uptown with their fruit jars of fireflies)	37
Rockefeller	38
The Answer To All Your Problems	39

Heimlich	40
Bridge Traffic	41
Punk	42
5,4,3,2,1 Blast Off! (and let the games begin)	44
The Sunshine State	45
Worse Than One Of Those Prank Phone Calls	46
Ole Factory	47
The Secret Art Of Exhibitionism	48
Just A Little After Midnight In Brooklyn	50
The Daughter Of A Specialist	51
Like A Fish Out Of Water	52
Common Scents	53
Social Work: Fall River, MA	54
Healthcare (if you dare)	55
Baby Jesus Flying Down A Slide In The Suburbs	56
Existence In 7 Shots	59
How The Chicken Crumbles	61
How To Self-Regulate Through Days Of Melancholy Like Feeling Like A Hollowed-Out Conch Shell In The Middle Of The Evening Blowing Your Shofar Slowly	63
The Past Tents And Present State Of The State Of The Job Market For Acrobats, King's Fools, And Philosophers Right After The Fall Of The Roman Empire	64
Fellosophy	65
Kids Watching "The Kid"	66
A Postmodern Hx Of America	67
The Common Cold	68
Lenny Bruce	69
Sitting With That Pretty Young Girl In Her Red Velvet Vest At That Cocktail Diner On Avenue A In The Lower East Side Gabbing Forever Under Overcast Skies 1:23 In The Wintertime	71
The Secret Life Of Acronyms	74
A Place They Never Speak Of	77
No Such Thing As A Midlife Crisis	78
The Revolutionary War	79
News From North Country	80
Talk Of The Town	81
Postcards From The Northern Plains	82
The Spirit & Beauty Of Social Studies	84
This Film Has Yet To Be Raided	86
On The Density Of Tumbleweed	87

Mantra	88
Single Cell Organisms (or a scientific study of suburbia)	89
Establishing A Baseline	90
Wired Around Twilight	91
Somewhere Between Midlife & Postmortem	92
The Theater Of The Absurd (or reality)	93
Tech No	94
Reality (or the theater of the absurd)	95
The Ageless Male	96
A Disrupted Sleep Cycle	97
An Addendum To Midlife	98
The Secret Art Of Lounge Singing	99
Social Work	100
Off The Strip	101
Ex In The City	102
tV	103
Suicide Postcards	104
On The Soul (Now You See Them Now You Don't) Of The Used Car Salesman	105
A Blueprint For Insanity	106
On The State Of Secretaries & Suicide In Fine Overflowing Rivers Which Run Through Town	108
The Punchline To The Eternal Miserable Riddle	109
One Of Those Advertisements Not Sure Whether They Are Asking Or Looking For Work As If Any That Really Matters	110
Patients	111
On Applying For A Position As A Recreation Coordinator At A Mental Health Hospital And Other Letters: found poem and sign of the times	112
Random Stanzas Having Something To Do With Manifest Destiny	115
The $2 Theater In Hell's Kitchen	118
How Barnes & Nobles & Bed Bath & Beyond Make Up The Perfect Life-Cycle In America	119
Pomp & Circumstance	120
Speaking To A Machine At The DMV	121
The Lost Art Of Bellydancing	122
Dwelling At Dusk	124
The Ending Of Summer	125
How Escapism Is As Much An Exact Science	126
Pics Of Your Hippie Mother In Backyard Full Of Marijuana But Always Took Care Of Us With A Good Sense Of Humor	

Slightly Overexposed Due To Time And Sun Over Her Shoulder	129
Ma Dear,	130
An Abbreviated Hx Of Ancient Civilization & Contemporary Society All Wrapped In One Somewhere Around Dusk	132
Right Around The Bewitching Hour	134
Preaching The Gospel	135
Driving Down Country Road At Dusk Before The Interview	136
Feed Animals (wife & kid summer service)	137
Nanook	138
Heaven Just A Keen Memory	139
A.M. Radio	140
On The Secretive (Not So Secret) Symbolism Of Soulmates	142
The Original Madame Tussaud	143
Right Around The Break Up	144
A Forgotten Amerika	145
Somewhere Between Fate & Mortality	146
The Secret Life Of Skywriters	147
Wouldn't Wish On My Worst Enemy	148
The Olive Garden	149
Land Of The Free	150
Something Like Faith	151
Global Warming	152
Just Off Walden	154
Whore Frost	157
Where I Live	158
Downtime	159
Breakfast Of Champions	160
Paradise In 6 Easy Installments	162
Suicide Tries Really A Desperate Stab At Life	166
Where The Wounds Begin	168
The Cost Of Living	170
Traveling	174
The United States Of America	177
On The Nature Of Porn & Weather	178
Infomercials: one's mortality in modern times	179
Ready Or Not	183
Getting Ready For The Upcoming Mosquito Season	184
Your Love Boat Crew	185
Situational Depression	189
Might Call This A Might Over Right Manifesto	191
Post-Trauma	193

On The Hx Of Real Estate	194
Ventriloquist Found Guilty In Murder/Suicide	195
For Armageddon...	196
An In-Depth Didactic Case Study Of C. Stooge	197
On The Origins Of Kojak Or The Nature Of First Love	198
Twin Portraits	199
Reservation Not Required	202
Saints & Hoboes	203
Blues: Or One Of Those Shell Games	
You Play On The Avenue At Your Funeral	205
Land Of Palm Springs	206
Munchausen	208
How To Soothe A Savage Beast	209
Moon Pie	210
Tradition	211
American Hx	212
The Smell Of Downpour	213
Living The Life	215
On The Essence Of Light	217
Domestic Violence: a love sonnet	219
Charlie	224
Plant City, FLA	226
Like Screaming Plankton	228
Mock Apple Pie	235
Kinney Drugs: the life cycle	243
Friendly's	244
Wanda	245
The Complaint Department	246
The Ancient Lagoon Business Park Of The Future	248
On Darwin, Or Plankton And The Origins Of The Ecosystem	251
Wendy's	256
On The State Of The Game	258
A Different Sort Of Manifesto (manifest destiny)	260
You Got Me Babe	269
Maturity	270
Stanzas Of Youth	271
A Bio Starting Somewhere From The Middle	274
Schmuck	275
Mental Health	276
Stand-Ins	277
Hospitality	281

Have A Cigar	282
The Graveyard	283
Overcast (with a chance)	284
Sans Title	285
For W. Burroughs	286
For stein, gertrude	287
Addendum: on the lifelong life of g. stein & alice b. toklas	288
for Nietzsche, Friedrich: an ancient hx of the contemporary world	307
Waking Up Dead Alone In One Of Those Gigantic Champagne Glasses Full Of Bubbles	309
A Natural Phenomenological History Of Planting	310
Dear Protocol...	311
Not In The Job Description	313
Just A Little Higher Than Higher Education	315
Ghosts	316
That Fleeting Forgotten Period	317
That Phase Which Never Gets Mentioned	318
Home Economics	319
Hypnosis	320
Scenes From Inside The Origami Bomb	321
The Colonel's Best	322
Walmart	323
The Lack Of Influence Of Media On The Lacking Individual	324
That Pretty Poor Girl From Illinois	325
Need That As Much As I Need A Head In The Hole	327
Somewhere Around Yonkers	329
It's A Story...	331
Guest Villain	333
What's In A Name?	334
Only Red White And Blue I Ever Worshiped	335
Clint Eastwood	337
Moving On Up But Not Quite Exactly	339
That Missing Piece To The Puzzle	341
Florida	342
In Apropos	343
Tick-Tock Of Cats & Smokestacks	344
Tally-Ho	347
Holding Your Breath Above Water	349
Domesticity	350
Vitamin C (and the case of the harassing fraud inspector)	352

Make Hay While Rome's Burning	355
5:35	356
For e.e. cummings	357
The Ancient Contemporary Pyramids: Somewhere Right Around The Reservoir Or How To Do Underage Drinking & Make Something In 3 Unequal Parts	359
A Slice (with nothing i mean everything on it)	363
A Tourist Guide To Nodding-Out	366
How To Not Lose It All (and regain perspective and be reborn) In The Bathroom Of A Sunoco	369
The Weather	370
Sears Roebuck	371
Wake-Up Call	372
Department Zero	373
Pain Killer	374
Right Before They Walked On The Moon	375
Coping & Survival Skills	377
Third Cousin To Caligula	378
After Confession	379
Boogie Wonderland (what it means to be a man)	380
Dusk Radio	381
The First Snow On The Mountain On Top Of Hospital Hill	384
Falling In Love With That Fine Country Girl With A Good Head On Her Shoulders	
As Humble As Pie Right By The Meat Aisle	386
Early Noon After The Deluge	387
Right Around The New England Doll Factory	388
I Think My Wife Would Be Far Happier If I Was A Big Bottle Of Blue Cleaning Fluid	390
Making The Scene	392
Vinnie Barbarino	394
Something Like Redemption	396
The Secret To The Secret Of Buried Treasure	397
After A Rough Night Of Dreaming	398
Cult:or	399
Insomnia –for g. stein one more time	400
Ambiance	402
A Mild Case Of Disassociative Fugue	403
A Botched Life	404
Putting Together A Badminton Set With A Passive-Aggressive Divorcee Talking About Lobotomies And Electric Shock Therapy On Memorial Day	405

Creature-Feature	407
Ho-Jo's	409
Before The Invention Of Paradise	410
On The Origins Of Drinking & Dart Playing	412
The Rest Of That Song Heart & Soul	413
Internal Organ: how the end not too far from the very beginning	415
Just Like One Of Those Streams Of Light Which Comes Out Of The Projectionist Booth On Some Dim Overcast Day	416
The Female Clown With Man Problems & Mean Pastor With An Attitude Taking The Hospital Elevator Up To The Solarium Soulless Going Through The Motions Forgetting What Their True Job & Purpose Is	417
Rawlings	418
Acknowledgments	421

"Among other things, you'll find that you're not the first person who was ever confused and frightened and even sickened by human behavior"

The Catcher In The Rye —J.D. Salinger

for dad
with love & affection

How I Been Getting By

like one of those film noirs
        with a sense of humor
where everybody
        gets murdered
that's how
        i'd like
to start this...
        & seems
the most
        accurate
& appropriate
        as everyone these
days just seems
        so full of shit
& only get back
        to you in your
obituary.

On The Domestic Front

How to eat a wolf sandwich
where out here in the illusion
of the suburbs rumors are real
life, and real life, non-existent

in desperate need of a
healthy dose of howling...

```
He Be Jesus
```

For me think it has something to do with global warming
or just way too much time on our hands as can tell us they
can tell us what Jesus looked like as a kid, or real-life pics
of Shakespeare. For me I just find it challenging to creep out
of bed on a daily basis and when I do, look like one of those old
ancient orthodox rabbis nodding-out in front of The Wailing Wall.

Soulmates

Yet once again insomnia and there you are once again
naked in front of the refrigerator downing cold smooth
milk hoping to make everything better and there's
that man again on the television selling some roto-
cleaning contraption which will hit every crack and
fissure of the bathroom to hope to heal your damaged
soul (the grand metaphor and parable for it all for all
things turned rotten and old) and always some english
man with an english accent and wonder why they ship
them in at 3 in the morning and what part of england
they get these psychos from and think does that make
it all that much more spiffy and sophisticated for all
us poor long-lost stranded souls at 3 in the morning
and wonder why they're only on 3-5 in the morning
and think it's for this exact selfsame reason to hope to
heal the beaten and weary and that very specific population
and demographic deserted and damaged by living every long
lost soul all those single women who deserve so much better
who have been cheated on one too many times before and now
just searching for some sort of father figure all those who never
even met a single woman all those with drinking problems all
those who suffer from nightmares and insomnia but interestingly
enough after having guzzled that cold milk and having watched
him muted on your bright tv screen do actually find yourself
slightly beaming just a slight bit better even a little reborn
healed and redeemed instantly feeling that strange feeling
of what it feels like to feel happy with that half-crazed
englishman with his english accent at 3 in the morning
having cleaned that whole damn sink and shower of
that milf just conveniently lurking over his shoulder.

Melancholia

In the morning, you wake up to your life story on the kitchen
counter which is a bill from "Presidential Pest Control," spittle
still in your stubble from the nightmares from the night before;
the weather woman with a seductive sardonic smile holds a whip
in front of a map of The Americas while right around this overcast,
dreary time of year, have made it a tradition to call up *The Von Trapp
Family Lodge* to ask for a job as have multiple years experience and
far more charm than the whole fucken lot of them or at least all of
human resources, or those gossiping snot noses at the front desk,
convinced you are being blacklisted, more accurate, at this juncture
just refuse to fill out a new application every six weeks, while know
the views are so much better from here so fuck 'em edelweiss
farewell goodbye to ya! and ya! and ya! You glance back down
at your life story and in the notes it says has replenished traps.

In the bare blustery purple mountains can hear in the
distance the oil trucks start to come in for the season.

Rosebud And The Smallprint Below

Other day i saw with some idiot caption
on the weather channel before they broke
for commercial which seemed like the classic
microcosm for all of america said something
along the lines of *town lifts ban for snowball battles...*
and then showed this quick-action shot of all these
children in this very controlled and contained area
tossing snowballs at each other and instinctively
the first thing that came to mind was yikes you
gotta be kidding? how this childhood custom
and tradition they turned taboo and forbidden
those sentimental moments and remembrances
where you spontaneously just decided to pick up
and pack all this snow together and with a sense
of whimsy and liberation suddenly watch it sail
through the air without a care as some sort of
seasonal ceremony at some pal or rival or even
girlfriend and pleasantly out of tough love or pure
glee waiting for their act of revenge so this is what
it's all come down to having to know those exact
specific places and areas and institutions where
it's okay and legal and won't be condemned for
going through the innocent childhood ritual of
naturally and mutually throwing snowballs?

The Long And Short Term Goals Of The Pickpocket And Pot Of Gold At The End Of The Rainbow

And so *America Online* now tells us
that it's cheaper to live on some cruise
ship than some cities; imagine that?
as your neighbors might be some
people you actually respect like
the acrobats and aristocrats and
lounge singers and sluts in sequins
and gigolos and fitness instructors
and when they show up to your
porthole with your medium
rare cheeseburger can just
naturally tell them please
put it on your tab and
you'd die a happy man
just like fdr out on deck
all wrapped up in blankets
with no regrets having done
his best considering the harsh
elements and sailing happily
ever after to a sadistic sunset.

```
Plainclothesman
```

What a sad strange life moving from skyline to skyline

some salesman selling a specific line that he swears by

which becomes his heart & soul & how he lives & dies.

Everything becomes a riddle to the eternal punchline

making his quota using hand-me-down quotes

analogies & anecdotes he picked up in his years

on the road & to rope & hook his client

& try to take advantage & sell the product

goes over all the required mandated

bullshit & brainwash bulletpoints

in the hopes to strike a bullseye

(like some quasi drive-by shooting

to reach his targeted goal of proverbially

selling the soul to ameliorate & upgrade

all those empty vacant areas of the consumer's

life to make him less lonesome & conflicted

& desperately question the meaning & purpose

& mortality of existence on an everyday basis)

& inundates him with facts & figures attempting

to read his body language & economic situation

with his fly-by-night one-liners

like some traveling ventriloquist

with his faithful dummy by his side

or sleazy comedian or balding lounge singer

with his tip jar moving from lobby to lobby & town to town

where he literally knows the hotel clerks working the nightshift

(develops an intimate, business-like relationship) better

than his own wife & kids & if he gets lucky

gets to see them every other weekend who are

either driven & disciplined overachievers just like him

or self-medicating to keep the fragile delicate illusion alive

knowing they'll be no actual consequences to their actions

which almost becomes the fragmented metaphor for their lives.

At his funeral or in his obituary it reads like a list of

traits & characteristics by acquaintances who don't

really know him having hoped & prayed it all might end

like one of those boilermakers in a bar full of strangers

dropping that shot of bourbon into a mug of beer

& guzzling it straight down in order to feel no pain

& get away from struggling & suffering & finally be saved.

American Kulture

who came up with that idea to talk into the mouth of a clown
in order to order your cheeseburger and fries

and all excited can't wait to get to the other side but when you
do always act so aloof and apathetic

and just like everything else in this life with survival of the fittest
you just learn to get used to it

and remain charming and polite and even compartmentalize
and look forward to that cheeseburger and fries

until you get about halfway down the road and look down
into your bag and see who got the last laugh...

Truffles & Ticking Bombs

Hear the mailwoman putt-putt
putting outside my window hoping
she delivers those truffles to the wrong
home again; do they still deliver bombs anymore?
i sure as heck hope so and want to be considered
significant and not important enough where someone
perhaps like some past perfectly unpredictable girlfriend
who didn't end well decides just during one of her erratic
mood swings to simply deliver a ticking bomb to my door
while i open up those truffles delivered to the wrong home
again by that fine incompetent mailwoman who refuses to
follow up and pick them up and after one of those long
miserable days on the road and just don't give a fuck
anymore unwrap each one one by one by one by one
taking in their delicate taste and texture and turn on
the television comforted by all the corruption and
scandals in washington and around the world and
right around when i'm like on my seventh one unwrap
the other one and go what the fuck and off goes that
ticking bomb with my body parts and truffle wrappers
scattered all over the floor which in many ways says it all

PS while eating them and really savoring them due to poetic
license and this fucked-up existence have this fleeting thought
that perhaps it's just the mailwoman who delivered them on
purpose and refused to pick them up, as have spoken to her
before and have had a couple really good down-to-earth con-
versations and hoping i might just once invite her in when the
snow keeps on piling up over the lousy left over pumpkins
up here in the mountains to try and make sense of it all

Any which way, at least with both, will go out with a bang...

The Hx Of Cinema In America

In between the small
talk bunch of sucker
punches & studs
& schmucks
fighting over
barbara
stan-
wick
inn...

A life
of leisure
half the time
they were drinking
& the other half
after their hang-
overs sobering
up recovering
from memory
loss coming
up with their
grande con
clue/gins

All that
struggling
& suffering
to live happily
ever after really
a cross between
illusion & deluge
inns of grandeur

(No matter
the staggering
salesmen still
throwing loose
change at the exact
same girl in sequins)

A Distorted Different Sort Of American Dream

1

that girl who lived double lives gave the best blowjobs

2

my god if i was to be interrogated by my ghost in candlelight
i would do just fine as would know how hard i tried
and suffered and struggled my whole life

3

interestingly that feeling of feeling
what you think it feels like to feel in love
is so much more than the actual factors involved

4

call me a male chauvinist pig
but in my opinion the greatest
diversity is in women's bodies
getting off in orgasm taking
a couple shots of pillow talk

running onto shakespeare's rapier
not really seeing my life pass in front
of me but the trailing sound of lounge piano
with no need to be judged or saved or redeemed
simply the silhouette of william shatner singing blowin in the wind

5

oi vei when you look at your tv screen
practically everyone is either holding a gun
or some sort of smart phone i suppose providing
some trendy sense of belonging and honestly not sure

if all this crap is some sort of new video or formulaic film
and i tell you if an alien was to fall from outer space either
landing here or the middle east he would instantly think
we live in a far more fucked-up and violent society

6

the half-crazed ushers know so much more
than the aloof & obnoxious know-it-all owners

7

the paperboy has been provided
a map of all the known pedophiles

8

the owner of the creamery
builds his spoiled daughter

who can do no wrong and a ho
a home right on the parade route

9

after your nightmares you go through the ritual
of wiping yourself down (like a clown taking
off his makeup) with a moist towel

like at one of those ole time chinese restaurants
and are able to return to sweet slumber like under
the shadows of a sputtering chandelier in a ballroom

10

escape door to the moon...

11

the lone tugboat captain and his fine relationship
with the phantom who provides a beacon from
the lighthouse and drawbridge operator
who lets him into the kingdom

12

he eventually is able to save up enough
to live in his dream home in the suburbs
right next door to the ruthless drug dealers

13

you have developed something of a rugelach
problem and now have to go to one of those
anonymous programs where against your own
will and volition you stand at the podium in
front of a whole crowd of other rugelach
abusers who chime in unison–"hi joey!"

14

turns out ironically this is where
i find my connection
for homegrown.

The (not so) Secret Formula

I don't know...
it seems like every
thing these days in
america is trying to
get to the bottom
of some punch
line while most
of them don't get
it and some do
and walk to
the other side
of the block
whenever
they see
me i see
some caption
beneath that milf
katie snow on msnbc
which reads 'arch
die o seas of los
angeles teaching
undocumented
immigrants to
not be deported'
i think they're
being serious?

Amerika The Beautiful

1. new details surface on the california bar shooting suspect

2. texas judge who lost re-election freeing defendants

3. the new victoria secret look for the season

4. what we have to look forward to in our future
   are discounts seniors didn't know they can get
   and show pics of row after row of mcdonalds
   fries and a close-up of one of those softee
   cones and think that doesn't look half bad.

```
How To Swim Safely Around A Nuclear Missile
After A Test Launch With A Couple Cute Rich Girls
From The Island You're Trying To Get With Or At
Least Store Safe & Secure In Your Jerk-Off Folklore
```

America has become just one big
gigantic stunt and cartoon character
crashing through our screen via vin diesel
and "the rock" right around suppertime
dodging perfectly choreographed cars
happening to be conveniently lit on fire
in mid-flight and this is all we have
to offer our children? the bottom of
the screen tells us we just dropped
our latest and largest non-nuclear
bomb in afghanistan like something else
we just casually did with our downtime

Some casually-dressed naval engineer
posing leaning up against it with a grin.

Those Treasures Found At The Bottom Of A Box of Cereal

I wonder what it was like for those first postwar americans
when they first moved to those lush suburbs i mean what was
it like when the wife had to find that first supermarket and
go shopping for tv dinners when her first horny son stuck
pin-up models to the wall when the daughter declared all
out war driving the jocks crazy seducing them making
them fall in love with her and instantly broke up with
them when they got too close when the delinquent
boys hung out all day at the pizza shop and nice
sicilians treated them like sons suddenly feeling
guilty and empty and hollow in an existential
panic at sundown and taking off like tarzan
with a monkey on his back through short
cuts to do homework and abide by that
cliched collective unconscious proverb
of making a name for yourself while most
of them just seemed brainwashed as coin-
cidentally just a couple years later would
see their expressionless expressions distant
and down in the dumps through the window
of the train on the platform commuters strangers
with that absurd awkward look of eternally lost
i guess having had made names for themselves

You think back to that pizza shop with those
nice sicilians who treated you like a son...

A Case Study Of Werewolves

1. Remember those pale-blue dungarees
   with the red bandana patches on them?

2. That suburban girl neighbor with the long flowing
   chestnut hair you dreamed of on top and below?

3. Peddling home from the pond after dawn with a best friend
   with no fish on the line feeling like you captured the world?

4. You were the real-life skull of the king's fool in school
   having sacrificed your heart & soul and paid your dues

5. When you get older you sleep like a werewolf
   and if you get lucky dream back to childhood.

Bowling For Dollars

i was found coiled in the fetal position
of one of those ancient arcade plastic
capsules tumbling out the bubblegum
machine outside a suburban supermarket
on a fine spring day in the late 60's
stuck deep in the pocket of a pair of
blue jeans with sewn patches on the
knees of a bright-eyed, wide-eyed, rosy-
faced boy open for anything with a vivid
imagination of mischievous innocent
curiosity tumbling over overflowing
muddy brooks in the back of toy
stores deli's and ymca's back to
the plush dead end of madness
and miracles with the scent of
sacred suppers seeping from
the screen windows over sun-
scorched porches...the sonny
& cher show may have been
tony orlando & dawn on
the *zenith* television.

Blueprint For A Life Of Leisure

Remember that opening
where mary tyler moore
on a pure whim
just flung her hat
up in the air some
where around some
pond in minneapolis
(i wonder how many
takes that took?)
i always mistook
her for "that girl"
as suppose it just
had something to do
with their similar optimistic
outlook on life. now i just
kind of find myself lost
like maxwell smart stuck
in that out-of-order cone of
silence searching for the button
or key to the lock in that fogged-up
snowglobe of orson welles trying to
figure out where it all went wrong?

The Life & Times Of Goofus & Gallant

Goof,

I knew my life was starting to go down
hill when we no longer were ordering
a regular slice but a slice of sicilian
and moved to the good side of the
tracks and there was no turning back

Gally,

I've had frugal friends growing up who would like not add ice
to their soda cuz they said could get so much more or when
mcdonalds came along with that once a year $1.00 deal for
a big mac would buy like 20 of them and literally freeze them
like roadkill in their freezer or at bar-mitzvahs declare out loud
to their mom–"make sure you get a gift from everyone!" and
these always seemed to be the ones who not by coincidence
made it while i'm ironically in the present empty and vacant
still searching for that pot of gold at the end of the rainbow.

A Missing Stage Of Evolution

Remember all those cassette tapes
we used to make and put together
with scotch tape with great passion
and perseverance and diligence and
meticulous teenagers in the seventies
and how they would get damaged
and the magic marker would run
from the sun all those neil young
albums with wasted lyrics and
the rhythm of brilliant tribal
native-american guitar which
would help you forget it all
and you know looking back
nothing meant more hearing
and trying to decipher waves
of it warped from the beating
sun in many ways kind of
wasted yourself already
from the unneccesary
stress and madness
of existence when
all you could really
do was look forward
to the future maybe pick
up a dime bag for later
on in the evening to make
it all go down that much
more easy–"comes a time
when you're drifting, comes
a time when you settle down."

The Anatomical Structure Of Flight

1.

why do birds have the desire to sit on a wire?
why do dogs go barking at sundown?
that whole ceremony of seagulls lined up along shore?
why do tree frogs come out after a storm?
why do cats go tip-toeing along the keys of a piano?
what happened to that pure myth and folklore of childhood
which just suddenly disappeared like the dew off the petal
of a flower from the mystical morn to the flux and industry
of what it supposedly means to be a responsible grownup
as if that spirit and those keen senses got kidnapped
by some criminal-thief-phantom but will never ever
give up which will be all those things we sentimentally
spiritually look to gain back in the form of romantic nostalgia

2.

in your bout with insomnia or perhaps just the real world
you see over your tv screen where they project *campbell
soup* will lose earnings in the upcoming quarter and how
it will have some sort of ripple effect as never been
much of a businessman, but think why not instead
just tie up and sell off that wicked ceo or executive
who resembles something of a sleazy diplomat or
politician you just do not trust and cannot relate to

and the beat goes on as you swear you see the price
for silver and gold and soybeans and porkbelly go up

3.

how about the price of a good redemptive rainstorm
or a friend you can trust and believe in
who might keep their word?

did we ever learn to be fluent in humanity?

Briefcases, Mulch & Garage Door Openers

i remember when my wife
the angel that she is
would throw me
birthday parties
& would invite
acquaintances
& colleagues
from my
mental
health
clinic &
from our
dead end
& used to
think, most
likely didn't
think it then
damn these
are my friends?
how depressing
& used to just
prefer getting into
in-depth discussions
with our babysitters
finding it far more
stimulating with
far more substance
& meaning, even
taking strolls
down that
dead end
taking in the
transcendent
scents & senses
of the mercurial
seasons hungering
for those days
of those
secret places

of those
tree houses
chatting
& dreaming
& planning
adventures
with kids
i had far
more in
common
with &
returning
home
at the
end of
the day
feeling like
a far more
complete
& content
better man.

```
Life Insurance
```

That little schmuck salesman constantly obsessively mowing his lawn like some mechanical robot always with his temper-tantrums and stare-downs due to consistently interpreting situations wrong like the world owes him something with his literal napoleonic complex and feeling insecure and not knowing himself who proves in fact to be a compulsive liar who can never admit he's wrong (when it's so easy to tell the truth and rather take every other coward option, life & times of the grownup in america) like some petty asshole sibling who finally confesses to you he's always hated you and betrayed you because he's always been jealous of you and nietzsche-like you're like what the fuck did i do this life insurance salesmen who makes every neighbor around him miserable and uncomfortable and if was to just stab him in his heartless heart and soulless soul and no one was around to hear it would he have existed at all?

Bet your bottom dollar bleed that invisible ink or not bleed at all...

Wichita, KS

she got so good at those pompoms
   used to just see her jumping up & down
on her trampoline, mechanical, magically
   with those mickey mouse ears on
right above the hedge of our backyard
   she got so good at those pompoms
used to just see her peddling that *schwinn*
   bicycle, hysterical, happy as can be
up on top of that banana seat
   intimidating all the cars
like some half-crazed dog chasing
   all the garbage men down the block
she got so good at those pompoms
   used to see her blowing past our window
during one of those great big biblical storms
   & all the men had their binoculars set on her
instead of the twister in the not too distant future
   she got so good at those pompoms
used to just see her robbing the local drug store
   with a stocking over her head & gun
& go 'there she goes, she's at it again'
   she got so good at those pompoms
would just simply knock over the fence
   dividing her lush lawn from ours
& never a word was said
   she got so good at those pompoms
used to take advantage of you under her porch
   where you got your first glimpse
of the female form
   leaving you in shock, startled & in silence
just wanting to return home for supper
   she got so good at those pompoms
used to just be found in very strategic places
   like right by our milkbox, our mailbox
by the blow-up pool, by the treehouse
   & turned out was my first love in one of those
polaroid shots looking like some hot femme
   fatale just holding her ground
you didn't want to mess with
   in the land of wichita, kansas.

Days Of Polaroids & Arlo Guthrie

Book me at the stagecoach inn
no one goes to anymore along
the very old commuter route
beneath mt. tittywhistle in
the berkshires which always
had that great big roaring fire
and onion soup and canard à l'orange
and flank steak and fresh warm chocolate
pecan pie; put me in that room in the back
of the inn right over the clanking kitchen
with a view of the mountain when all
goes dim and all may be forgotten.

Before & After (The Captain America Action/Adventure Existential Version)

Those damp skeleton leaves
falling past the drizzly windy
lattices of anti-bellum mansions
on st.charles avenue, new orleans
could you really be that lonesome
starving, forgotten, sweat-stained
shirt soaked to the bone until
you finally feel so perfectly alone
alas no one can possibly know
you, except yourself, hollow
& wholesome, racing your
rattling bicycle against those
languid, lumbering streetcars
of bleak beautiful & bizarre
madness taking on some
whole other surreal reality
with suicide ideations
the routine & ritual
of what it feels like
to be eternally empty
& abandoned
the ship in a bottle
the human cannon
ball passed down from
generation to generation
butterfly kisses of phantoms
the banging of shutters in the
screaming shattered nighttime
only thing keeping you alive
only thing keeping down lies
only thing keeping you out
graveyards & mausoleums
on the tips of the holy
& haunted wings
of the gargoyles & seraphim
the sweet scent of magnolia
& crepe myrtle while murdered
without even knowing some

time ago; your flickering
stirring soul in the storm
like a beacon in a shattered
window, delicate, incandescent
glowing, the senses that much
more lucid & illuminated
a saint & a thief slipping
through the keyhole of
the lucid wallowing seasons
between the dusk & evening
between illusion & reality
between sanity & insanity
somewhere in the subterranean
labyrinths barely surviving between
magazine street & the mississippi
in the sweet splendor of squalor
where all history started
& the future ended.

`Like Hot Air Balloons Taking Off In Tornadoes`

the truckstop whores knock on your door
                      while you're in the moonlit berth
                                              spooning
the gravestone salesman's daughter...

is this what they meant when they said–
got to go through hell before you get to heaven?

Civilization 101 - 101

I returned to my apartment today to find some
dope addict had broken in and was just casually
cleaning the crumbs and boloney and chinese
off my counter; he was scrubbing each piece
of silverware i had once purchased at *woolworth's*,
swept up all around my futon on the floor and naturally
declared–"sorry, i just couldn't rob you, and just felt
like you may have needed the help more than myself
...how do you even expect to have a girl over here?"
as guess just had never ever noticed or even thought
about it and was simply living my life and surviving
on a day by day basis, and suppose what i learned
from this was that we all just suffer without even being
aware of it and the little tiny details which really make
the difference; i thought about pulling out my checkbook
and writing him a check but thought that might be over
doing it and do more harm than good (and what would
that really be teaching him) so decided to just offer him
a cup of coffee and simply shake his hand and thanked
him for breaking in and paying a visit, and led him back
out to the fire escape where he disappeared into thin air.

Wasted

Spending those long sweltering
        summer days out in coney island
                the pure blissful madness

of the puerto ricans & sicilians
        on shore
           the stories
                (& punchlines)

    they told
        for the whole wide world to hear
            without even being aware of it
                (very aware & thriving off it)

getting suntanned,
        buzzed,
             burnt,
                wasted

                returning back
                    to your hovel
                        in brooklyn

to mad wild echoing of alleys
        of hustlers & delinquents
            & scents of spanish rice
                & fried fish

                removing the clothes
                    from clotheslines

  & taking apart
the last of block parties

        listening to wu-tang clan's
            first hardcore album
                nothing then could have felt

                                        more liberating
                                        & independent
& sacred
& of the core essence...

AP: getting ready for graveyard shift
at *the pioneer hotel* in the heart & soul
of chinatown & little italy when pee-wee
the old merchant-marine nightwatchman
for no apparent reason would suddenly
in the wee hours of the evening let out
this great wailing madman howling shriek
like one of those ole lowdown haunted fog
horns creeping in from shore & wake us all
up out of the nightmare we were in & every
thing life had done to us up to that point
returning back home when that tired
drunken sun with a hangover came
up over the old red brick drowsy
tenements with the early dawn
dewy glistening fire escapes
& ragmop leaning over dripping
drip drip drip like some ancient
slapstick comedian slouching
fast asleep with a grin on the train
having missed his stop ages ago
& you go staggering back to the
subway bleary-eyed & beat a
former ghost of yourself but
somehow in one full holy
complete piece similarly
dropping dead on your futon
on the floor content & at one
'cuz really not dreaming at all.

```
Lullabies (or the brothers from uptown with
            their fruit jars of fireflies)
```

It's always the guilt which gets you in the end
yet still have absolutely no idea what you did

like the relationship between a dummy and his
ventriloquist in front of a performance which

keeps on getting postponed and decide
to go fishing instead right around midnight

by the burnt-down coliseum where the comedians
and angels and out-of-work actors roam

sharing a cheeseburger and fries
at some all-night boxcar diner

with a flaming redhead just as down
on her luck and deserted as yourself

knowing that everything really
starts right there from the middle

right there in the moment
after all the bullshit betrayals

while it was always your rapport with
the rivers with the silhouetted mountains

nocturnal creatures of the silent forest
which were like flickering beacons

that got you back
safe and sound.

```
Rockefeller
```

Today the wife and I drove all the way out to the posh part
of Vermont looking to purchase a Northern Red Oak and came
upon one of the most beautiful, breathtaking views I have ever
seen, I swear perhaps in all of The United States of America; of the
misty, ethereal, rolling folds of the faraway Adirondack Mountains
looming over Lake Champlain, while she happened to be in one
of her very vindictive, ridiculous, domestic violent moods, as felt
resentful that she had to drive all the way out there with me and in
a classic petty power-struggle almost refused to look out at them
and take them in and see that they even exist, like some opposite
proof of man, but wouldn't let her ruin my moment, and after
this long journey one of those seething snobby higher-than-
holy horticulturists (I guess after a lifetime of dealing with the
obscenely wealthy and wannabe aristocrats from the suburbs,
obscene in the most prudish and predictable of ways) who seemed
something of a real man hater, forgot what they're called, but know
there's a definition, and has some preconceived notion before she
even gets the chance to know you, and have to prove yourself by
probing and asking sensitive thoughtful questions and talk circles
around her, and upon bringing up this recent sweeping scene of
looming majestic mountains, suddenly told me that Rockefeller
had purchased the view and kind of knew exactly what she was
referring to like she was trying to impress me with this quixotic
and perplexing statement, which intended and implied how no one
could ever put up like some condominium complex or business
park or golf course, and thought goddamn god bless old man
Rockefeller; they really in fact sincerely just don't make them
like him anymore...

When we got home she got me back
by disinfecting the whole house.

The Answer To All Your Problems

You know your life's pathetic and petty
when you go on *facebook* (something
you haven't done in ages) and look up
babysitters; the ones you had for your
self and the ones you had for your kid.
Isn't that the way they taught us how
to figure out the median in grade school
and pile them all on top of each other
and take the one right in the middle
and thus there lies your answer?

Doesn't life/loneliness in the long-run
just seem like still apologizing for
some joke you know they just
don't get trying to make you
feel eternally like shit?

```
Heimlich
```

You always wondered what went on during "suicide watch"
and who does all that watching or is it just some punk or
schmuck as indifferent as the rest of them getting paid
minimum wage and wondering could you like order
in take-out and then when chowing down one of
those happy chow fun sweet & sours or number
7's or fortune cookies when they're not looking
probably making some inane small talk with another
pathetic apathetic nasty nurse or reading some gossip
magazine slip out into the evening hell i've even called
the hospital up on top of hospital hill and left real nice
polite messages for human resources to become a
patient sitter who never get back to me (which only
confirms to me all of humanity) and even got a d
gree with more experience "far better" than them
i always wondered what suicide watch looked like?

```
Bridge Traffic
```

t. sawyer
    drained, wasted, tired
      or as the brothers stated–
          "just trying to make it"
      dials
        "1-800-LAWYERS
              The Heavyhitters..."
& thinks to himself humble
    as pie just stolen off the sill
        don't need a heavyhitter

              just need someone
                  to finally trust
                      & get me out of this

    there's a cathedral...

    right next door to a factory
    right next door to a laundry
    right next door to a prison

where in the window
    like the lower east side
        on rivington
            a slight candle sputters.

Punk

Still waiting for that infamous ghost elijah
        who we always left the french door open
                for/eign that broken dusk garden
                            in long island
to show up
  to scoop me up
      to sweep me up
          to spoon
              my shivering
                    shattered bones
     from all those
phony promises
                of betrayal
                    made like
                        johnny rotten's punch-
   line–
     "ever feel like
         you been cheated?"
              knowing johnny
                  you're just being coy
      when said was just
          being rhetorical
              as literally know exactly
                    what that feels like
i spent my down time
      in malls
          on the out-
  skirts with my fellow delinquents
        ripping the sensors off
                  of books
                & ralph lauren polo's
     putting my whole half
          way drained
        heart & soul
              into it
  for presents for passover
      with the adrenaline
        on-the-run
            get in full closure

                                        & pot sublimation
elijah where are you?
    "it's 10 o'clock do you
            know where your children are?"

5,4,3,2.1 Blast Off! (and let the games begin)

When I woke up from a bout of insomnia I dreamt
I looked into the bright blue sky of the television
like a kid from childhood gazing into the reflection
of a puddle at one of his toy rockets blasting off
to the heavens from another nuclear missile test
from that Napoleonic spoiled brat toy soldier from
North Korea while during the hotdog eating contest
in Coney Island on the 4th of July our wigmaster with
a toy cannon of his own pointed at the sky decides
to retaliate with a try (and trial) of his own and
the whole fate of the fucked-up free and unfree
world depends on the moods of these madmen as
all of World War III begins from the absurd temper
mental temper-tantrums and grandiose delusional
disconnects closed-up hearts and souls and cruel
brutish dysfunction of megalomaniacs with very
poor self-images and fragile identities and egos
(and the rest of the 'she loves me she loves me not'
humanity made to existentially and psychologically
and spiritually suffer like some Kafkaesque torture)
all off those old time glossy posters of propaganda
shrunk down to size in the postcard carousel
of the Lilliputian lobby of some grande hotel
chock-full of toy soldiers, politicians with
their token conspiratorial briefcases, parrots
of multiple-personality disorder having escaped
their cages, an undercover dummy-ventriloquist
act dressed in disguise as dictators, and a lounge
singer at piano taking requests for bellicose blasts
from the past, finally, at last, from the tongue-tied
tourists playing roles of all-you-can-eat aristocrats.

The Sunshine State

I tell my wife sometimes even scream aloud
am i speaking another language sometimes
i just think i'm way too nice to them while
she does her best job possible at being a real
good wife and providing the best validation
something like i always tell you joey you're
just too nice and friendly and think they just
end up taking advantage until i end up ironically
hollering at the top of my lungs i don't know
any fucken different! sometimes when i'm
real desperate think maybe god is just sitting
back up there looking down on me from his
velvet throne and having one hell of a good
time chomping on his popcorn with the extra
butter asking the concessionist this indifferent
teenage chick snapping her gum is this real butter
or that fake coconut oil thriving off all my problems
and suffering and sorrow like the job description of
one of those ole time slapstick comedians who some
how through their slipping and sliding made us feel
just a little bit better in our wretched lives maybe might
even help us to forget for a short time and get by but
say no that just can't be he just can't be like everyone
else and will naturally and instinctively look up to the
ceiling and then just feeling cursed and like it's all a
bunch of bullshit nod-off in front of the weather channel
watching 125 active fires burning in the state of florida...

Worse Than One Of Those Prank Phone Calls

Called my local *rite-aid* today as my prescription
had run out for tylenol and they had that song
i think from the eighties think it was what they
used to call power ballads and had to listen to
something that sounded like this melodramatic
shit 'motor end what's your price tonight?' and
had absolutely no idea what they were talking
about and was such boring and bizarre lyrics
i couldn't connect with or make any sense
and could see why back then i was always
depressed. when that missing-in-action
pharmacist finally got back on who was
pretty damn short i asked him if he might
possibly just have anything a bit stronger?

Ole Factory

Doesn't everything from school daze
stem & stray from fluff & peanutbutter
sandwiches when you really think about
it i mean smell i mean think about it not
doing your homework hanging out with
your pals and mad handmedown bicycle
at the pizza place during the dusty and
desolate draining dusk in the she loves
me loves me not stripmall on-the-run and
how you did at recess rounding the bases
for another spring is busting out all over
homer with a hole in your jeans and
skinned knees and heart thumping
dreaming of your future all coming
from the stray scent of that fluff &
peanutbuttter sandwich stuffed
in a brown paper lunchbag...

The Secret Art Of Exhibitionism

1

Crows in top hats & tails taking ballroom dancing
through the lit florescent windows of upper broad-
way at 8:23 on a mad sweltering summer evening

2

The young girls have stripped-off their clothing
showing off their ballerina bodies putting their
scent out there during the season of seduction
something of a reverse hibernation and tradition
in this quixotic city of ambiguity and anonymity

3

Out-of-work actors come out of alcoholics anonymous
with their raging histories of histrionics, explosions, and
accusations playing starring roles of dr jekyll & mr hyde

4

Divorcees sit in windows of cafes, casually stalking
their prey, trying to land a guy; their only criteria of
course being that of money the exact thing that got them
into this whole mess in the first place at a very young age

5

The old doorman with a dry sense of humor
who has won over all their trust, and makes
more of a connection than most of their family
members makes a good living due to union wages
and seems to know more than all of them put together

6

The orangutan scratches his head next to the little kid
having a temper-tantrum whose dad is a workaholic wall-
streeter and wife taking up stealing (for a living) with onset
tourette's making very obscene and overt comments with
references to their sex life in public from a lack of intimacy
when running into friends and acquaintances at the whitney

7

Soon will finally be autumn and that stray sacred
scent of chestnuts in the sputtering solemn season.

Just A Little After Midnight In Brooklyn

with windy
blushing
cheeks
i see
all the
universe
from atop
my mid
night
stoop in
brooklyn
not a soul
around just
silhouettes
and sound
of that slight
stray breeze
of whispering
cymbals
fluttering
through
the sheltering
shadows of
blustery
trees
and only
when
i'm
sure
it's all
settled
and calm
do i return
to the moon
in my window.

The Daughter Of A Specialist

I love the writing of ernest hemingway but i guess
don't so much like that he was apparently something
of a rabid anti-semite and would like refer to salmon
as 'the jew fish' and so on, and as tanya harding put
it–"that's just rude" so hemingway this one is for you
and when i die fantasize to be a very large salmon perhaps
behind the counter of "tal's bagels" in the upper east side
where those really gorgeous down-to-earth looking jewish
girls who claim to be zionists but suppose truly are neurotic
would ask to have me sliced a certain style, most likely
very thinly, and then open me up gingerly and gently
and very selectively pick me up, and toss me over a bagel
on top of a nice dietetic smear, focused, fixated; toss their
long dramatic wavy hair to the side and when they imbibe
have something of an orgiastic feast of me wherever i
happen to be right there on the spot and the whole
world stops at tal's bagels in the upper east side.

Like A Fish Out Of Water

One historical fact that in fact no one knows about
that in the signing of The Declaration of Independence
someone suddenly shouted "Oi!" and George Washington
standing in front of the congress angrily exploded–"I want
to know who said that! I want to know right now!" Benjamin
Franklin frankly and very meekly stood up and hesitantly
responded–"Alright, it was me...But I was only kidding...
Can't you take a..." and before he could finish his sentence
George Washington in that infamous pose he's so famous
for standing stoically at the edge of his boat while crossing
The Delaware, what we now see on every *Howard Johnson*
and *International House of Pancake* placemat declared, while
pointing–"I want you out of here! I want you out right
now!" –"But...but George...come on, be a sport, it's
raining like hell out there" –"Out!" and about five minutes
later with the rain coming down like cats & dogs and the
lightning lighting up all the panes of Philadelphia Franklin
drags himself in, drenched from head to toe, while sulking
goes–"Guys...I think I might have discovered something?"

Common Scents

not so long ago
when a pair of
rollerskates
in a shag
carpet
closet
and a girl's
bright white
ice skates
hanging
around
the door
knob
meant
so much
while a
blue fog
crawled
past the
vestibule
window
before
school

now they check
their smart
phones.

Social Work: Fall River, MA

the nuns were fun
in the chart room
of insane children
who were removed
from their homes
for things done
wrong to them
and had a good
sense of humor
and were in touch
and pretty down
to earth and
do think could
relate to me cuz
saw me as some
thing of a badboy
just like them
who had been
around the block
in a town
in a city
which didn't
have a whole
hell of a lot
to do with
virtue
or sin.

Healthcare (if you dare)

nymphomaniac social worker
as cute as a button flirting
madly and intensely
with me across
the table at the
treatment plan
meeting never
quite sure what
they want from
me because know
we're both married
but looks so desperately
and sincerely and wonder
if she just got into a fight
with her husband and had
it and just using me to save her
that's usually the way it ends up being
having something to do with their identity
wanting to feel attractive again or loved
or someone listening to them and my main
concern always is what are their plans after
the one-night stand? guess you'd call this
something of a treatment plan as always
said the clinicians i work with far more
mad than any of the actual clients or
kids who were put there for reasons and
circumstances far beyond their control...

Baby Jesus Flying Down A Slide In The Suburbs

People forget about
karlows dostoevsky
the bastard brother
to fyodor like the
infamous sister
of the kennedy
siblings who
they got rid
of because
of her a
parent
uncontrol
able id &
fits of rage
& ain't
sanity
& sent
out to one
of those
shock
factories
the rage
of the day
no return
to sender
no rsvp
somewhere
in the dakotas
or the midwest
where they
teach you
to repress
& forget
& artificially preserve
& not make trouble
for their reputation
this too happened
to lou reed when
his hardworking
jewish parents

found out he
most likely
was ex
per i
meant
ding wit
his sex
yawl
i dent
ditty
& jolted
him with
a couple
thousand
volts from
the hard
land from
the heart
& soul
of their
safe &
secure
sub herb
from thee
shag rug
of early
sixties
long
island
imagine
that parents
making a
decision
like that
because
of some
thing
like that
& might not
have gotten
that brilliant
thought pro

voking yo
deling mono
tone mellow
dramatic haunt
dead album
where war
hole did that
cover with thee
banana of thee
velvet under
round & nico
nicotine teen
star of tv stars
factory fairies
pure porn stars
who found dead
unearthed & dis
covered amerika.

Existence In 7 Shots

1.

i got into a brawl in one of those gondolas
on the *mr. italy* mario perillo tour and they
sent me back home all by my lonesome
to laguardia in my ten-gallon and my
parents mandated i see a psychiatrist
who kept on wanting me to take an iq
test cuz saw me as some kind of genius

2.

funny i saw right through him while he ironically
eventually, ended up breaking confidentiality
they were all such a bunch of fucken phonies

3.

how to let love back in your heart
like some balding lounge singer
with a drinking problem
playing his electric piano
in the airport lounge of
key biscayne, florida

4.

do the russians also do
poisonous darts and imagine
wonder woman deflecting them
with those bullet-proof bracelets

5.

triggering memories and recollections
of best friend's divorced mother's stash
in a little sandwich bag in her night table
rolling it up with the sticks still in them
in the rich poverty-stricken section of
the upper east side of manhattan with
the electric flames from the romantic
fireplace nodding-out to all-night cable
of topless hosts with their tits hanging
out getting bored and eventually switching
to midget wrestling returning home wasted
bleary-eyed on *the metro north* in the morning
for some pathetic very mature disco pool party

6.

their marital problems always solved
coming down the winding stairs
at the end of "the love boat"

7.

putting all your faith
into tattoo & mr. rourke
passed-out halfway through
due to boredom seeming like
the great metaphor for it all...

How The Chicken Crumbles

last night hypnotized
      in front of the refrigerator
with insomnia just staring
            at a leftover bucket
  of "the colonel's best"
        with his infamous mugshot
stamped on it & noticed it
      read something like
            "raised on u.s. farms"
  & thought what were the other options?
the moon?
   honduras?
    some laboratory?
       & found myself
         entranced & transfixed
             with this sudden
               very strange & profound
                   motto & message
   just printed on the side
       of this great big bucket
          as if under the influence
of the very far left
     or the very far right
        or very patriotic
          or just a very necessary   &
obligatory
     statement printed
        by 'big brother is watching' f.d.a.
             anywhichway it seemed
                to do the trick
   & get my mind off it
       like some beacon
           or piece of pop art
              getting my mind off
                  not being able
                     to sleep at night
   "raised on u.s. farms"
            with leftover extra-crispy
                crumbs

pretty much
what my life has become...

How To Self-Regulate Through Days Of Melancholy Like Feeling Like A Hollowed-Out Conch Shell In The Middle Of The Evening Blowing Your Shofar Slowly

they got no idea and will never
have any idea what it took to
climb and finally get to the top
of the mountain while sometimes
i'll just sit back in the morning,
grateful, thoughtful, contemplating
the blessed, brooding, sky-blue ribbon
of mist and fog, bending, blanketing
winding itself around the body
of pines, sprinkling the tips of
branches and eventually vanishing
into the foot of the forest; i'll even
look to the tippety-top at that one
single one at the most tippy-top
whose sacred, silhouetted skeleton
transcendently etched against the clouds
almost seems to silently scream aloud–
look i made it! nothing can stop me now!

a bird with his back to me
brooding on the wire, minding his
own business looking out to the horizon...

The Past Tents And Present State Of The State Of The Job Market For Acrobats, King's Fools, And Philosophers Right After The Fall Of The Roman Empire

how the flowers of the lower east side used to smell like
drizzly dawn after driving a yellow taxi all night long
brown paper bag full of fried gizzard and hot sauce
and sports headlines missed the night before all
washed down with a *ballantine* beer paying your
dues living over *selassi i* where the rastafarians
who i liked used to supply me discount bags
of hawaiian gold during another long sweltering
summer which somehow seemed to save my soul

Fellosophy

they never get back to you
a proof of their pettiness and
non-existence and what actually
makes you stronger and wiser
believe it or not less loneliness

stuffed derma left over in the fridge...

```
Kids Watching "The Kid"
```

Wow! the kentucky derby being ridden already again
finally at last winter's end and seems like just yesterday
stevie cauthen they called "the kid" mounted that gorgeous
steed think was only like 17 when he won it all so damn exciting
so damn wonderful wasn't just on the edge of our seat but had to
stand up for superstitious reasons and watched it all from my pal's
home in the suburbs and how quickly time and life just seems to fly
by just like that 2 minutes time...

River raging across the road from all the snow melt and rainfall
blue and holy and sparkling and flowing into the mountains
only thing that really makes me feel alive in this existence

Ironically it turned out to be quite a muddy race
while in fact just didn't matter who took first place.

A Postmodern Hx Of America

1. the indians were actually the ones who kept the pilgrims alive
   helped them to survive and could have taken them out any time

2. jump to marlon brando in *the wild ones* supposed
   to be a rebel and wasn't crazy about him in that one
   as found him to be obnoxious and in many ways
   subjugating and just as guilty at being a thug

3. we now have an all-knowing omniscient idiot commander-
   in-chief a nice return back to royalty where he is simplistically
   deciding on the spot like switching the tv channel who's allowed
   to stay and who must go

4. i sometimes like to think of the thought pattern of one of my
   clients with asperger's and wonder if all of america will just one
   day turn to video and the television will read "game over" and
   wonder if anyone would even care or notice like some school kid
   who's supposed to be cool and curious and now can just stare
   down at his smart phone to cross the road like some real life
   (really not so much...) demented riddle and joke

5. i wonder how many of my facebook friends
   will show up to my funeral?

6. sluts in the mall and old men passed out by the fountain
   of youth waiting for their wives to return
   from the department store...

The Common Cold

all these posers and wiggers in america
where the hell did they come from and
when did that all start and can we just
send them back to wherever the hell
they came from i mean is there some
place where they can all be deported?
is there some white trash motherland?
is there some father figure forgotten?
or maybe just one of those gigantic
dumpsters we can just gradually
push them in and squoosh them
when they ain't looking? would
they be o so scary and o so intimidating
then with their pre-manufactured anger
and perfect o so attention-seeking wannabe
cookie-cutter monochromatic pose leaning
at the perfect angle behind the wheel of their
car (pretending to be some big time gangster
but most likely a little man with a little mind)
most likely picked up from mtv's "pimp my ride"
heading back to their mommy's house in the same
small town (the same small town mentality and same
small town suburb) they grew up in a perfect pretend
generation of selfies and self-important assholes
who just seem like they're trying way too hard.

Lenny Bruce

he survived that gigantic hook in vaudeville...
he survived all those sniveling snotnoses in the catskills
he survived the cheap plastic covered furniture the borscht
& gefilte fish poor taste rigid ruled customs of impossible
to please grandparents from the old country who sincerely
believed that passed-down cliche better to be seen & not heard
he survived the kill van kill river which runs filthy & vulgar
unsung under all those unknown brokendown bridges
of the bronx & harlem
he survived all the lies & betrayals & bullshit of human nature
& turned it into brilliant solipsisms & soliloquies of sublimation
he survived the machinations of the devils & angels constantly
gnawing at his bones until all that was left was the heart & soul
he survived the sticks & stones of the mean-spirited & mediocre
& mashed it all into the mortar & foundation
of a far deeper & diverse culture & civilization
he survived & fought against a brutish & barbaric
cruel & cut-throat system which turns out when you
get down to the nitty-gritty just another form of fucked-
up democracy from judge to policeman to beat reporter
who when they can't beat him (beat him) & act together
like a bunch of cowards to ruin & destroy reputations
he survived the slings & arrows of the coward critics
he survived the pettiness & persecution & prisons
of a kafkaesque kangaroo conspiratorial court system
he survived living off the side of a milk carton as a kid
all the poor school teachers in the nyc school system
& being a wise ass who couldn't stay out of detention
he survived multiple marriages & multiple divorces
he survived all that bad coke & heroin & angel dust
from los angeles
he survived a real life (not really) bullying blacklist from
the brave men in blue & a sexually-repressed government
bent to pay him back for free expression & telling it like it
is & the natural consequences of gee whiz little white men
with napoleonic complexes stemming from fragile identities,
hostile, passive-aggressive, petty & trivial, all those things
which get the philosophers & poets & prophets imprisoned
he survived the character assassinations of a mad insane

generation but i guess the thing which got him which gets
them all in the end is all the gossip & rumors from a civilization
he once considered a friend all that bullshit guilt & conflict like
some uncontrollable propaganda of the subconscious (a collective
unconscious who picked up their bags & deserted & abandoned)
something like insomnia or some existential empty nest syndrome
really having no other choice but to become a soul survivor an
innocent & defensive son of a gun & when he just couldn't fight
them anymore had no other choice but to turn it all on himself.

Sitting With That Pretty Young Girl In Her Red Velvet Vest At That Cocktail Diner On Avenue A In The Lower East Side Gabbing Forever Under Overcast Skies 1:23 In The Wintertime

it's the city
that scares us
it's the city
that doesn't
it's us!
it's us!
it's us!
it's us!
let's rip off
our disguises
& discuss
our self-disgust
our reasons
to exist &
not to exist
in this rare
rarefied
starving
lunch hour
moment
which brings
a strange
liberating
calm to
all the chaos
to all the lost
loneliness
to all hour
blues in
the hush
in the lush
ashes to ashes
of dust to dust
somewhere
between
the factory
& funeral home

& cafe & church.
when they're done
he simply pecks
her on the cheek
outside the park
as if thanking her
for filling in (letting
go) of all that built-
up strange bullshit
redundant rhetoric
& now finally at
last forgotten
foreboding
emptiness
which vanishes
into thin air just
like everything
else that just
picks up
& leaves
for no reason
out of nowhere
& hasn't
quite been
discussed
but felt &
shrugged
off in the
moment
all that
leftover
knit-picking
all that borscht
& bone soup
& spitting
up blood
sacred
self-effacing
lingering
& looking
to be saved

now just
simply
crumbs
the core
rhyme
& reason
flickering
reflection
which once
was some
obsession
that now
means
nothing.

The Secret Life Of Acronyms

I.

It's not really so much a matter of domestic violence
being 'brought up' on charges of domestic violence
a form of domestic violence, cuz if you only knew

how petty & trivial & absurd & ridiculous it was
a power struggle of semantics & body language
& expressions & the redundancy of existence

if you were only a fly on the wall of domestic violence
makes the battling bickersons look like saints & doves.
need multiple personality disorder to survive marriage

our problem these days and know might even sound a
bit cliche is that we have absolutely no heroes anymore
no one to look up to, no one to turn to, or fall back on
they've been gone way too long several decades or more

you got kids addicted, clueless, codependent
who can't get off their freaken cell phones
nor care to see anything around them
in the real world literal state of denial

acting all self-important, brainwashed, believing
that this is what it is that makes them belong

our professional athletes are multi-millionaires
strung-out on performance enhancing drugs
and our politicians well won't even go there
as pure satire and cartoon characters

(so who are the real criminals
and what in fact does dv stand for?)

as really not so much a matter of domestic violence
but more so something rather foreign and unfamiliar
with no clear translation and far more
in the category of an existential crisis

II.

I'm not a believer in them
but for those of them
who are ufo's always
seem to just show up
when you got nothing left
to lose nothing left to live for
in the real sweltering weather
some time in the summer
usually got no girlfriend
with a lot of downtime
or way too much time
on your hands with a
hell of a lot of masturbation
& a very specific plan
so all pretty random
feeling desperate
& damned
taking a final stab
somewhere between
land & the constellations
returning home late at night
from the club, blasted, buzzed
that beacon over your shoulder
like a prayer like a street lamp
like a boxcar diner somewhere
around the bridges & graveyards
& mantras of bullfrogs & cicadas
your refrigerator with simply
cheese & bread & seltzer
& that *arm & hammer* just
as much a loner & lifelong
companion like some lit
screen in a bleak drive-in
which only proves how
much you've seen &
how much you haven't
schvitzing in your rental
on the lake in the mountains
those solitary nocturnal creatures
& mailbox full of arrest warrants

which you haven't checked
in you don't know how long.

A Place They Never Speak Of

that pink house
at the end of
the bridge
with views
of the lumber
trucks the women
hitchers and the river
when it just begins
to flood its banks
this is the land
boys work all day
take cigarette breaks
and casually hang out
in their bloody aprons
maybe for just a couple
spare extra bucks to pick
up a 16-pack at the *shell*
station or a painkiller
here and there from
their much older girl
friends slurring their words
not sure who's taking care
of who with the holy mist
slipping down the mountain
mixing with the early morning
smoke of smokestacks and
chimneys of cozy shacks
on the outskirts of town
filled with brothers
and sisters and
not a mother
or father to
be found.

No Such Thing As A Midlife Crisis

That lonesome wound nurse who lives up in the high mountains
who wraps my leg up in a cool and healing adhesive gauze and
i rest my foot up on top of i imagine her naturally bringing it up
just below her bosom and up a little further and caressing and
going back and forth over her blessed sagging breast barely
brushing titillating her nipple causing her to let out a slow
seductive sigh unable to catch her breath which actually
ironically proves to heal and be cathartic in everything
in her cursed existence that has so unfairly deserted
and abandoned her as of recent then delicately buttons
up and mechanically very casually mentions–"i got you down
for next friday at 9" as you simply reply–"i'll see you then…"

```
The Revolutionary War
```

I need a sketch artist on an everyday daily basis
who will flesh-out all my moods and very fragile
state of mind and existence and will fill up his
tip jar to the top with loose change and maybe
if i get lucky will take requests; one of those
damaged entertainers whose women all left
in some insane, half-crazed lounge constantly
experiencing drama and crisis night in night
out; some old laughing hag smoking cigars
rocking back and forth on the porch with her
escort gangsta' black man under a bugzapper
beneath the stars then return casually back
through deep dark woods of glowing eyes
of nocturnal creatures cautiously creeping
out of revolutionary war graveyards just as
lost and lonesome as myself to that window
on the lake where my much older sugar baby
unconditionally waits and welcomes me naked
while always ready who once claimed she didn't
want the relationship to get too hot and heavy and
when you finally have had it and have to hit the road
starts whelping out loud how she knew her dogs were
gonna make you go while you naturally immigrate back
to the city and her to that commune of pretty whimsical
windswept women wailing in creaky caravans on the sea.

News From North Country

The bright-eyed buxom broadcaster in thick makeup
her mother never quite taught her to brush on correctly
suddenly engulfs and swallows up her fellow newscaster
boring the hell out of us with his very choice and casual
small talk, while we see his slim health club figure naturally
moving down her trachea, letting out a slight burp, and with
a little giggle peeps–"O excuse me" and very matter-of-factly
says– "And now for our North Country weather" where another
very slim prudent, neat and tidy man in his conservative glasses,
pretending to be all nice and kind, whimsical and funny, responds–
"Thanks Jenny" and watches his back now a little more guarded
and discreetly, while pointing to different regions with captions
flashing beneath him about school closings due to an impending
ice storm, at last moving towards the last story of the morning
where they display like one of those idiot reenactments of some
Revolutionary War battle where they show a bunch of old timers
and bankers and accountants scuttling through the suburban
forest all dressed up in their tight Revolutionary War uniforms
made to look like Minutemen, like during one of those school field
trips you used to take as a kid you loathed and hated, which
would bore the hell out of you (thinking more so about getting
laid and all the classes you were falling behind in) with resentful
maidens getting paid minimum wage to make brooms and butter
while the camera finally pans at last to that buxom bright-eyed
broadcaster just standing there with her poorly brushed-on
make up and her plastic, psychotic smile, feening, standing right
next to the last remaining, slim, very flamboyant newscaster
cozying up to her due to apparent natural consequences
and her might-over-right mentality, acting all happy,
getting ready for a new day up in North Country.

Talk Of The Town

My wife got a shot of this lone moose just clomping
all through downtown this morning and told me how
she heard they just like to walk casually through the
center of town as if just a part of the crowd without
a trace of being self-conscious maybe even window
shopping past the bookshop, the jewelry store, the
bridal and barber shop, the cathedral and coffee house
and thought wouldn't you if you were coming out of
the deep dense woods during the winter to a bunch
of young women just gossiping about how they've
been continually cheated on by lousy men with the
luscious warm aroma of omelettes and hashbrowns
seeping through the grates of the corner diner
and ornery judges in the window?

Postcards From The Northern Plains

Out here in america
they show over the news at 7
               "the children's shooting club"
   & a proud 7 year old
with rifle & camouflage

        while just over his shoulder
            in the back of a pickup
                that poor dead deer

                  with its eyes
                        glazed over
                        gazing up
                        to the heavens

    & such beaming parents
            taking his photo
                    with a smartphone

while my son's best friend
        mother who believes in the cause
                drives 72 hours straight

     from vermont to north dakota
          stops over once for shelter & support
                            in chicago

& by the next day
      bleary-eyed makes it
           to the campgrounds
           of cherokee country

getting chased like that deer
through the prairie trampling
the shivering cold november
rivers protesting the oil lines

           being *put down* beneath
                sacred indian ground
                    ("and the beat goes on")

    with the very brave sheriffs
  spraying mace
& wooden pellets

    at them as interestingly
       like no footage
          from iraq or afghanistan

this never makes the news and wash
off their wounds at the indian casinos

       2 blushing blondes
       (beauty salon style)

       without a care in the world
           go back & forth

  over the local news with giggles
  & inside jokes about the weather

       hx has a tendency
         to repeat itself

      but who the hell would know
         or for that matter even care?

The Spirit & Beauty Of Social Studies

i swear it they don't make explorers
                          anymore standing
                                    all bold
        on the edge of precipices
                looking out over the whole
                                blessed sunset universe
    the very brave & courageous
              lewis & clark
                    who took off
                          on their journey
  from the east coast over the mississippi
                splitting-up getting lost
                          in indian country
              until finally after battling
              the conditions & seasons
              they miraculously heard
              like a revelation
     through the lush trees
the lashing crashing pacific
                imagine that
                    who was that
                          who stood up
       around upper-manhattan
        around cloisters
               looking over all the majestic hudson
    (the hoodlums
        in the heather garden)
was it hudson?
    magellan?
      or was magellan
          just the mississippi?
                to me none of that
                    really matters
                        just the silhouette
of one of those
      long-lost brave souls
        looking out over
            the 'brave new world'

AP: any which way something i'm sure of they don't make explorers like that anymore just a bunch of fucken brainwashed imbeciles looking down at their smartphones not seeing a single thing around them.

This Film Has Yet To Be Raided

i was thinking today and know may sound cliche
but still blows me away how we made extinct
the whole breed of wild buffalo on the plains
and almost the whole american indian race

like the image of that hollering spoiled brat obnoxious
kid from "where the wild things are" to a grownup
version of charlton heston lifting his gun above his
head in proud protest as the president of the n.r.a.

i spew in the bathroom of the stripmall laundromats
which now pumps out less soap to make a couple
of extra bucks controlled by the cosa-nostra

and return to my motel room
just outside reno to am radio.

On The Density Of Tumbleweed

Down through the old rundown motels
where the valley of the main drag dips down
below the dusty keyhole a river always flows.

out here the blessed beaming clouds always hang low
this is the land where the traveling circus got its start

& those like moses, clint eastwood, butch cassidy
& sundance, billy the kid, joe buck & ratso rizzo
all had empty & vacant & broken hearts &
never ever really wanted to be on-the-run

that was all made-up & romanticized & just wanted to find
that idealized place in the sun, some promised land
to rest their bones & a place to call home.

prayer was all that stuff leftover
blowing somewhere between
self-defense & survival
in the fleeting moment.

Mantra

ricepaper biplanes
coming down
in the paper
mache fog

i love the melt off
of winterspring dusk.

```
Single Cell Organisms
(or a scientific study of suburbia)
```

Proud milfs sit in the stands
of the little league world series
all sponsored by *gillette* razors.

On the day of the apocalypse
all we see over our television
are one of those game shows
with families standing opposite
from each other and the stud
game show host in his jet-black
toupee and *dentyne* smile holler–

"Let's play the feud!"

Establishing A Baseline

You wonder what it was like
that first day of life when that
amphibian crawled out of the
ocean to check out and explore
the shore to see what it was like?
was there some kid's bike laid
on its side with a kickstand
and rat trap and a drooping
clothesline in front of some
high-rise felliniesque condo
in naples, florida? you sit
back in your easy chair
watching the weather
channel high on pain
killer as she gives
a handjob to wichita
kansas which triggers
when that milf picked
you up at the movie
theater and took you
to the stripmall to pick
up chinese, whiskey, and
videos and take advantage
of you over the weekend
then dropped you off at
the burlington northern
where you crawled
bleary-eyed back
to portland.

Wired Around Twilight

I still haven't gotten to that phase in my life
in that phase of life where i might proclaim with
all my might like some shyster because he knows
he's squandered his whole life–"those were the best
years of my life!" or perhaps i have just forgotten and
in denial or just lost my mind and in that phase where
i'm just trying to get by or get through the day and most
of all the night like being towed everyday after work by
the same tow truck guy of who i have developed a fine
rapport with back home to a gorgeous radiant young
wife who waits worried wondering and actually acts
as if she really cares about me (lord knows why...)
in the kitchen light and a warm supper in the oven
and man is that not the best we can hope for and
ain't that what true love's all about what they're not
my dad the dentist wanted me to be a real successful
driven cut-throat stockbroker and my mom wanted me
to be a young clean-cut tony curtis with those gorgeous
glowing blue eyes and in both i failed with flying colors
i guess declaring in technicolor somewhere during
happy hour those were the best years of my life.

Somewhere Between Midlife & Postmortem

These days i find myself weeping
           for no apparent reason.
                    last night it was while watching

mash & hawkeye suddenly for the first time
became self-effacing & thanked frank
for his support & in my easy chair

simultaneously found myself
welling-up while eating macaroni
salad waiting for the sky to break open.

```
The Theater Of The Absurd (or reality)
```

When you think about the idiots and buffoons running the world
literally can't even get to the peace table without another insult,
murder, suicide bomber, secret missile test going off, like
jesus' last supper being replaced by a don rickles roast.

```
Tech No
```

during the holiday season always a trigger to
some form of depression you think up satire
that war can no longer continue in the middle
of the desert right in the middle of the middle east
because they run out of one of those triple-a batteries
the revolution cannot be started and televised in the cities
because the internet is down and cannot figure out where
and when to meet; likewise you are waiting for your internet
to get back up and just end up instead rapping in your hall
good ol' third bass and ll cool j "all we got left is the beat."

Reality (or the theater of the absurd)

These days in america you now see all the time
on your news channel one of those long tickertape
captions at the bottom claiming another mass murderer
facing the death penalty and the way our system is run
and botching-up just another execution, show him
instead in the penalty box during some hockey
game in the playoffs, of course when they interview
him he'll profess his innocence and claim something
of a mistaken identity, and give him a commercial for
one of those *icy hot patches,* sighting his jersey being
the no. 1 seller amongst teenagers; the other player
who leads the league in penalty minutes will count
down his days on death row as they're ready to put
a whole squad of deathrow inmates to death due
to some mad scientist medication about to be
discontinued and terminated; a couple years
later, that mass murderer will run for a seat
in the senate, as america of course famous
for its convenient amnesia, sense of forgiveness,
and sight absolutely no conflict of interests, turning
literal madman and murderers into missionaries and martyrs.

The Ageless Male

and so i'm just sitting there in my easy chair...
passed-out dead to the world and all of a sudden
comes on this commercial for "the ageless male"
where there is a similar selfsame figure just trying
to get some z's in the rays of his tv when suddenly
this blonde with this silly and seductive smile most
likely his wife shows up in her sexy nighty wanting
to get her needs met and i'm thinking am sympathetic
to this poor guy who's probably working at some job
he can't stand for some boss he can't stand and
fellow workers he can't stand and here he is now
drained dead to the world forced to have to perform
on demand and think i want to see the one where
he is sincerely passed-out laid-out on his bed but this
time from an apparent overdose with an empty bottle
of that ageless male and she shows up once again
with that silly and seductive smile wanting to get
her needs met and show her suddenly turn all
down-in-the-dumps disappointed and depressed
but decides instead what the hell why not give it
one more try one final shot one final fuck and peeks
under his drawers to find him much to her surprise
much to her good fortune and good luck still turned
on with a hard-on and gets on and gets off and the
camera goes back and forth between that expression
of him literally dead to the world and a bottle of
that ageless male which seems to say it all...

A Disrupted Sleep Cycle

in
  som
nia
is just coming
out the vagina
wailing cuz
frightened
and unfamiliar
with surroundings
but also instantly
becoming sick
of it all fallen
asleep inn
a swaddle
like being
tightly
wrapped
in a
rubber
stuffed
back in
a wallet
of a kid
just not
getting
laid in
college.

```
An Addendum To Midlife
```

ad. reads searching for...

"someone to repair
my jack-in-the-box
he won't come out

not sure if broken
or just simply
given up?"

The Secret Art Of Lounge Singing

who came up with that really obnoxious
spoiled expression of–"charmed, i'm sure"

sounds like the rapport of some
breakup with a borderline girl...

Social Work

i had to get her out
of her apartment
immediately...

the jesus loving
people had bedbugs.

Off The Strip

All this bullshit of american exceptionalism...
sorry but just get so sick of it and take exception
showing all these up and coming schmucks for
like *fairfield hotel* running up and down the halls
on the treadmill juggling balls, female ninjas
or some "expert" balancing all these different
sorts of objects as these are the guests they cater
to and want or if you show up you can be a part
and be just like them well how about the poor
souls with drinking problems, eating disorders,
bipolar, borderline, situational depression whose
features and symptoms often overlap and just cause
them to struggle to get out of bed? do they have
some hotel for that with acrobats doing cartwheels
and back flips in the lobby for them?

Ex In The City

i always hated those parts in those feel-good films
where the boyfriend was forced to meet her girlfriends
like some sort of fucken tribunal like who the hell are they?

i want to see the one where he meets them at some
beat-up bar and hustles them for a couple bucks
for drugs cuz he's feening and down on his luck.

tV

Satire is all we really got left when you consider
the nature of incessant shit they constantly spew at us

    You wake up in he morning to find out the president
of *bumble bee tuna* has been indicted...

```
Suicide Postcards
```

Sometimes you just get so lonely
you are not even aware of the things
(the people and places) which make you
lonely or for that matter know you're lonely

Depression's a strange bedfellow...

```
On The Soul (Now You See Them Now
You Don't) Of The Used Car Salesman
```

most bureau
crats are alley
cats but may
be i'm selling
them short
that being
the alley
cat as
there
sure as
heck were
some stray
dogs and
alley cats
i swear
i knew
from
thee
neighbor
hood &
board
walk
i trusted
& grew
fond of
& developed
a rapport...

A Blueprint For Insanity

i'm ready for when the cops come
to kick down my door maybe
with one of those 'all for one
one for all' battering rams
(bugles and blowhorns)
and go–"go cuff him!"
and you holler back
at them the cow
ard pigs that they
are as they had heard
a rumor from one of my
neigh/bores that i had had
fallen in love with a drone
missile and how i simply
just loved to cuddle and
canoodle and spoon
him and sometimes
even take him on
vacation with me
and strap him up in
the passenger seat all
the way up to pennyslvania
dutch country and always
seem to come zooming
through the trees hooting
and hollering overmanned
in their manned-up swat team
barreling through the suburbs
with nothing better to do in the
early late bleak afternoon and
always screaming too loud as
if trying to scare you and seem
like they're more scared of them
selves and they always tell you
to like sit on some stoop or get
on the floor which you always
resent and refuse to do 'cuz
this is your home and hate
you even more cuz you're

never scared and bold
and don't want to be told
where to sit or stand by
a couple of little clans
men who in your opinion
are just disturbing the peace
and just wanting to get some
piece of mind most of the time
minding my own business with
my downtime just imagining
puerto rican parochial school
girls taking off their uniforms
where you used to live right
around the heather gardens
up there around cloisters
no, i swear, nun of these
things ever really happened
and yeah i been arrested
before by these cowards
but for domestic violence
that they always created
as just didn't have the
courtesy or for that
matter the bedside
manner to ask nicely.

On The State Of Secretaries & Suicide In Fine
Overflowing Rivers Which Run Through Town

After a long impossible winter which never seemed to end
and with the melt off of snow into the swollen overflowing
rivers in the mountains i like to imagine just the tips of ships
peeking around the bend, the circus caravans coming rattling
in with their tents and neatly packed pachyderms and madmen
but there's not a soul to be found due to a plague taking out
about half the town and the other half having lost faith and
closed down, while torrents of rain come back around to
help to just forget it all and the movie theater opens up
again for purposes of healing, like some ridiculous insane
masquerade party where you swear you can hear in the faint
distance the wailing of phantoms and goddesses and even
secretaries in that constantly churning overflowing river.

```
The Punchline To The Eternal Miserable Riddle
```

A whole patch of sunflowers
growing up alongside the barn

you imagine are the classic ole time
comedians with their gaggle of squirting
flowers cracking us up and turning us on.

The help wanted ad asks experience
in driving a logging truck you picture
very much like driving the getaway car.

One Of Those Advertisements Not Sure Whether They Are
Asking Or Looking For Work As If Any That Really Matters

Looking for man or woman with lawnmower
who won't run over garden run over sunflowers
run over mailbox swear ain't making any this up

that their help just didn't show up or always needing
just that extra part spending more time with their built
in excuses than just doing their job constantly whining

and complaining and kvetching and charging respectively
(not too respectfully literal highway robbery) an extra 15
or 30 bucks (as have to get off the lawnmower) to weed

whack and get the trail through the forest
while ironically we're as nice as they come
and always pay them right on the spot

what happened to the ol'
sicilian father and son
team of lenny & ralph?

who was it woody allen
said 90% of it's just
showing up...

Patients

A whole holy day of shut-ups between the wife and i–
you shut up! no you shut up! you shut up! like a bunch
of fucken punks going at it practicing their declarative
statements yelling shut up at each other like a pack
of immigrants barely able to speak the language
conveniently knowing the pithy phrases slightly
scraping their fenders during their graveyard shift
stubbornly conjugating the only verbs they know
going– you stupid! you stupider! how all great
ridiculous wars started as well as ended like one
of those comics in one of those foreign language
text books while ironically barely understanding it
cuz suck at french and fluent in remedial showing
a cartoon with a caption of two limo drivers going
at it with the two separate affluent customers sitting
back as if nothing's happening and you wonder what
got you and your wife to this fatuous and futile fucked
up point anyway in the marriage both two very good
looking characters with a great sense of humor who
met in social work school in our second year of internship
on jerome avenue in the bronx falling in love slow-dancing
in our window in washington heights when the sun went down
and started beaming and reflecting right off that apartment building
right around cloisters not god forbid becoming just like everybody
else spending a full day of going back and forth with a wealth
of idiot shut-ups breaks my heart and can feel it somewhere
between the upper-chest cavity and where the words come
out as in this case the cliche really does hold true it hurts
me more than it hurts you or when it comes down it really
none of that at all rather the whole fucked-up principle of it all

Honestly i prefer it when she tells me gonna stab me in my sleep
at least a little more originality and not all that back and forth shit

I miss those tow truck drivers i used to have great rapports with...

```
On Applying For A Position As A Recreation Coordinator
At A Mental Health Hospital And Other Letters:
found poem and sign of the times
```

Letter #1

Dear HR:

Lots of love, never got a password!
And got to be honest besides your
fine bedside manner, and thank
you for that, this process has been
grueling and frustrating, as have now
literally gone back and forth at least
twenty times to your site just to try
and at least create a password so will
allow me to even move on and apply
and won't even allow me to do that
(that's why I gave you previous
consent and approval) as you
see I have a really decent and
experienced clinical resume
but to be brutally honest does
have something of a sincerely
torturous Kafkaesque Orwellian
quality! Will see you on Tuesday
and have a great weekend as well!

Sincerely Yours,

Joseph D. Reich, MSW

Letter #2

Dear HR,

I was under the under impression it had all been completed
filling in all that was asked, and what it was presenting
and felt like had finally gotten closure with what you
had received and our rapport; I have just tried to go
back again this evening, but to no avail; I really
honestly can't go back anymore, if that precludes
I cannot have an interview, please tell me and will
hold off on this process and all of this protocol...

Thank you much,

Joseph D. Reich, MSW

Letter To Self #3

Boy, what a cool Freudian slip of the tongue...
'under the under impression' with this maddening position
which has taken over seven hours to try and complete and
get up on my computer, not allowing me to create passwords
and so on to be a van driver to discharge and commute
Alzheimer's patients back home, which has caused me to
completely lose my patience and mind and become one, the nature
of the fucken times, and an MSW with multiple years experience
and clinical recommendations in the field; this also happened mind
you with The Trapp Lodge, that Austrian family you know who
somehow got out and escaped Nazi Germany, Edelweiss!!! i.e.
was tempted to write to head of Human Resources on Hospitality
Drive unit #324345 J. Reich head of Human Beings, but not so
sure if she'd "pick up" my Joyce &...

Confidentially signing out,

Joseph D. Reich, MSW

Letter #4

Dear HR:

Upon some reflection and even a bit of brooding yesterday evening, I am going to have to respectfully pass on the position; I did meet with the program manager, I believe a very nice English gentlemen, who was a real pleasure, and one or two others from t he clinical staff, showed up very diligently even early as always before the interview and before they were ready, was respectfully peppered with a number of different clinical questions dealing with situations and scenarios and crises and methodologies (and how they function and operate things with the clients, their eclectic backgrounds and how they work with the animals and chores on the farm and so on) and believed I thought to have answered the questions rather thoughtfully and insightfully, then after about an hour and a half, met with the CEO and had a nice casual rapport in her home for at least an hour or so just naturally peaking and exchanging life experiences, felt really good about the interview, literally got home about 9 o'clock in the evening, the wife kind of laughing with my son, that daddy's something of a schmoozer, but again not to stray or be too tangential, really in my opinion was not afforded the proper respect or in my opinion, professionalism, to get back to me at all to tell me of the status of the position. I followed up at least twice with the owner, even randomly about a year later, put in another cover letter with my experienced clinical resume just to inquire if any positions had possibly opened up or were available, and still never heard back, honestly felt just a little strange and quixotic, and something of a disconnect, did not internalize, just felt like well I tried, and so to me, honestly, would just be a little awkward coming over there again for another inter- view, having to fill out another application, putting myself out and so on, just wanted to afford you the respect and flesh-out and provide clarification to why at least at the present time, would just have to hold off on the process, I'm sure you understand being clinical and compassionate, and myself spending so much time thoughtfully sharing my personal and professional and clinical experiences, why instinctively would just feel something like a conflict of interests; thank you anyway and do sincerely very much appreciate the follow up...

Joseph D. Reich, MSW

Random Stanzas Having
Something To Do With Manifest Destiny

0.

Recently i've been sighing
like mr. kotter going
down in a plane
some yenta with
windows open
in the shtetl

1.

Our concept of birth in america
we're breaking up...we're breaking
up...steve austin...man barely alive
...we can rebuild him...faster...stronger
charlton heston falling to his knees
in his loin cloth...enough is enough
is enough...is.barbra streisand
donna summer...suntan lotion
with the paba...the ice machine
regenerating softly in the evening
on the warm buzzing terrace just
like paradise at the holiday inn

2.

Wife told me kids don't wear cords anymore
what the hell is this world coming to?
wearing those navy-blue or maroon
cords 7, 8. 9. 10 years old...

skidding after the ball at recess on the asphalt
on the sopping ballfield with mud and blood
putting a perfect hole right there in the knees
of those navy-blue and maroon cords...

3.

I always like on craigslist
when they try to sell like
some adirondack side table
in the middle of a lawn of
fallen leaves and always
think i'd like to just buy
that fall foliage scene
giving me a hankering
for an american cheese
sandwich on wonder
bread and butter

4.

I am moving to California and
getting rid of a bunch of things:

- Lots of folk music CDs
- Books
- Sample cosmetics (hotel shampoo/conditioner and the like)
- Safer sex supplies: individual condoms, lube samples, unopened
  packaged box of Today sponge (3 count)
- Random tchotchkes
- A pair of size 8 women's heels, black, in the box
- Record player
- Ostrich feather

5.

Blind slightly open
in the train depot
bringing in the
smoggy lights
& no one on
the platform
you fall back
asleep with

the ghosts
& phantoms
& will wake
up a new man
on the border
of denver &
the new world.

    The S2 Theater In Hell's Kitchen

jesus christ
lowers his
head in hand
in the cracked
mirror of the
snow globe
which shatters
into a thousand
pieces at the
ankles of
that genius
who did all
those film
noirs and
while on
your knees
holding on
for dear life
like brando
in streetcar
wail hysterically
still in love
with your
girl from
the bronx.

How Barnes & Nobles & Bed Bath & Beyond
Make Up The Perfect Life-Cycle In America

...starting from all those milfs to die for in the children's section
not knowing how young and fun and neurotic and good looking
and good sense of humor hippie mother wife of a dentist was
to somehow all of a sudden making it to judy blume's "tales
of a fourth grade nothing" making it to dostoevesky for extra
reading and loving the challenge as always wondered about
the thickness and identity of the brothers karamazov on that
spare and simple gold mustard cover to getting a little older
and becoming a literal hustler getting one of those what you
call frappucinno's is that what you call them putting in all
this free and downtime trying to pick up a girl and never
once getting one going one on one and returning home
all by your lonesome to your brownstone in carrol gardens
brooklyn which used to be the perfect family-oriented mafia
neighborhood and now cold and austere and no one
anymore hanging out on stoops anymore because
of very competitive yuppies from hell and up and
coming females in the publishing business who
know exactly what they're looking for to bed bath
& beyond potchkying and rummaging around trying
to figure out what you'd want in your fictional home
when you're all grown up and which one had the best
air-conditioning in manhattan when you're schvitzing
all the way to the afterworld suddenly realizing you're
so young when they first try to assassinate you in america.

Pomp & Circumstance

I got trampled and run over at one of those
all-out video game every-man-for-himself sales
at the mall and was like the running of the bulls
with very organized and single-minded teenagers
who had been camped-out the night before and
picked myself up off the floor all by my lonesome
bruised, cut-up, hearing the muzak version of *the four
seasons* through the 'big brother is watching' speakers
while staggering disoriented somehow making my way
back through macy's to the parking lot and took off
(knowing that by heart) from the providence mall
back towards the suburbs of boston where the
original statesmen staged their first rebellion

Actually consider myself quite lucky not to be a man
of the people or what they like to call them; individuals?

Speaking To A Machine At The DMV

After being held hostage on the phone by the dmv
with a mechanical machine they finally because of
"volume" or an "abundance" of phone calls gave
me the option of pressing number 1 which would
allow me to leave my name and information and
after not giving a fuck anymore and wishing i was
dead matter of fact think i may have tried to killed
myself was unsuccessful and then tried again told
them my name was elmer fudd i own a mansion
and a yacht then explained to the mechanical
machine i was only simply being sarcastic
'cuz they had me on hold for close to 20
minutes and after providing elmer fudd's
basic demographics provided them my own
and just wanted to know if i could send them
a personal check in the mail then proceeded
to walk down the hall where had a feeling i had
been through this exact thing before telling them
my name was elmer fudd i own a mansion and a yacht
and in more ways than not found to be quite cathartic
just not sure if i ever received that phone call back as
upon retrospect not sure if any that would even matter.

The Lost Art Of Bellydancing

After night in and night out wired and wasted
ordering the same take-out of pizza or subs
or chinese i decide to 'let my fingers do the
walking' and give a ring to get one of those
door to door belly dancers and she shows up
with great alacrity to my door under all her veils
and silk gossamer and asks in her broken turkish
or flemish or flamenco not sure which one–"are
you mr joseph?" and i say–"yes, i'm mr joseph"
as she proceeds to ask me very respectfully
and gracefully but business-like where do you
want me and she traipses up the stairs of my
raised ranch in all her capes and disguises
can even hear her cymbals and rings tinkling
and going off and plunks down her boom box
then asks me if she wants her to turn off
the weather girl and i tell her no that will
not be necessary and for the next twenty
minutes it's just me and her and the weather
girl having the time of my life in complete
ecstasy forgetting all the petty and trivial
bullshit and crises and conflicts and crime
of living interestingly fending-off what goethe
likes to refer to a 'trembling' or sartre as
'nausea' while she goes into her seductive
swooning and belly shaking and swiveling
gestures with the weather girl in the back
ground pointing her hand to the heartland
all having one hell of a time and swear can
feel all the tears and pre-cum welling-up
inside me and before i know it am in a
total state of relaxation and stimulation
explains to me that my time is up and
she's got to leave of which i totally
respect and don't want to take ad-
vantage or make a scene and ask
like after some decent sex making
if she takes personal checks and she
says with some hesitation in her broken

turkish, yeah i guess and then proceed
to give her a chocolate cake soaked
in rum that i baked and am famous
for and she says you didn't have to
as i naturally retort yeah no i had to.

Dwelling At Dusk

I just want to
grow eggplant
parmesan in
my summer
garden and
orange crush
bowery bums
doing their best
impression
trying to
get from
one point
to the other
how does
that equation
go again 'the
shortest distance
between two
points is a
straight line'
while doing
some stagger-
ing as well
my life has
taken on
a similar
like reality.

The Ending Of Summer

you turn your son on to ginsberg
a day before he goes into 6th grade
                             on wednesday

you ask him what he thought of him
& he responds amazing & is gonna
go back at least 2 or 3 times to read
"howl" & don't care if he's crazy or
insane & explain to him he's not &
all about expressing yourself & to
try "america" & "kaddish" as well

when the sun starts to sink over the barn
he vanishes to water the corn & pumpkins
& sunflowers & think what else can you ask
for with all your recent episodes of melancholia

you are excited that gorgeous latino weather girl
is back early from her maternity leave & can see
her ripe shapely bosoms beneath her black sweater
all filled up with mother's milk or liquid gold as gotta
admit & not one of those perverts kind of turns me on

he spends the rest of the evening kneeling beside your wife
who has passed-out as always in her butterscotch rocking
chair in the corner with the tv on a little tinkering away
diligent & industrious & building his leggo kingdoms

she gets up like a sleepwalker & naturally announces–
"i'm gonna have to fill out those lunch forms for tomorrow.
who knows? maybe it'd be peanut butter & jelly" & think
words of wisdom & a damn fine & good & decent way to
approach this ridiculous & godforsaken thing called living.

How Escapism Is As Much An Exact Science

if i ever get rich
yeah i swear it
am gone get
me an extra
apartment
in the lower
east side
& paris
& white
plains, ny
why white
plains, ny?
why not with
my suburban
lover just as
destitute
making
a spiritual
intellectual
connection
both just
as lost
& left
over
with no
direction
& her
shag
carpet
children
& our
secret
italian
&
sea
food
dives
on the
outskirts

of town
where
all we
know
are
the
night
time
fogs
& mists
& silhouettes
of bridges
& a little
further
up teddy
roosevelt's
boyhood
mansion
where he
used to
diligently
collect
butter
flies
& why
high
on fine
cheap
red wine
we'll plan
vacations
to reno
salt lake city
the dakotas
& northern
california
where no
one knows
us & used
to runaway
as a teen

ager slip
ping up
& down
the verd
ain't
narrow
down
pour
poor
down
rural
small
town
mount
tins in
my trailer
sacred &
anonymous
through
the key
hole of
sleepy
cabins
& shacks
& truck stops
awe shucks
there was a
reason why
in childhood
you used
to always
fall down
& look
for an
easy
way
out.

Pics Of Your Hippie Mother In Backyard Full Of Marijuana
But Always Took Care Of Us With A Good Sense Of Humor
Slightly Overexposed Due To Time And Sun Over Her Shoulder

    1969,
america

Ma Dear,

for our
christ
mass
card
this
year
just
wan
2 show
awe
3 of us
standing
there
dumb
struck
stone
faced
startled
staring
through
the blinds
of some
motel
watching
the hail
fall like
ping
pong
balls
into
thee
bleak
empty
pool.
who was
it used
to preach
there's
a time

and
place
for
every
thing
wow!
think
about
that
if you
trans
lated
it lit
rally!

An Abbreviated Hx Of Ancient Civilization & Contemporary Society All Wrapped In One Somewhere Around Dusk

She's the last
one in the fields
before the lightning
and thunder comes
while the misty fog
like firmament spills
down the mountain
and sprinkles
the corn
as she peddles
her bicycle home
in her blustery
sundress blowing
up from her butt
to her bosoms
and you suddenly
realize most of
your dreams
are crawling
on your hands
and knees just
trying to make it
to the promised land
you wonder how much
time groucho spent
and put in
to primping
and grooming
his fake bifocals
and moustache
the romans took
a hell of a lot from
the ancient egyptians
which instinctively
to me feels something
like an earlybird special
and sorry no disrespect
most of our politicians

these days resemble
something like straight
men with one-liners and
not an ounce of humor
while it appears most
of the department stores
you grew up in are shuttering
their stores due to a poor economy
getting back to that girl in the fields
they say i guess the equation for hell
has something to do with repetition
expecting that something new
or different will change or happen
yet think if ever get rich and realize
that illusory american dream
am gonna test its validity
and simply sit solitary
in some classy candle
lit gourmet restaurant
night in and night out
waiting on my blind date
the eternal romantic that
i am and turn that expression
on its head or that frown upside
down however the hell that goes
and show them what true love
is all really all about–

"Can you put it on my tab?"

Right Around The Bewitching Hour

Red tow truck
rambles through
the twilight lights
of boys looking
to get laid on
a friday night
with 16 packs
of beer; won't
even get close
and drunk, turn
brave and romantic
adventurous and courageous
end up wrestling each other
in the shadows, staggering
dropped off on dewy lawns
the best way to blackout...

Preaching The Gospel

Baby in the future please don't heap
all that shit on me in the morning
enough to make me want to take
a flying leap right out the window!

Buy a whole herd of alpacas without even asking...
kept the black gospel station on on the TV as those guys
really do know how to get it all out and weep and wail and
somehow keep you alive when you feel dead to the world.

Driving Down Country Road At Dusk Before The Interview

you see that alpaca with his head cocked to the side
as if brooding and befuddled after the storm

the *sears* truck is lost going back and forth
over the covered bridge under the miraculous purple
clouds of the mountain looking to deliver a refrigerator

girl's lemonade tables have all been collapsed on the front lawn

boy all decked-out in his baseball uniform
weeps in front of a farmhouse

hostile businessmen return home to the suburbs

wild golden apples glow during sundown before you reach town

strangers and young lovers exchange secrets around the lake

after the interview you take in the soft glowing light of empty
rooms behind the country curtains of solitary homes and
the sweet smell of burning cedar streaming from chimneys

at the change of season which will always no matter
where you are lead you to your destiny...

```
Feed Animals (wife & kid summer service)
```

1. put cat food out for cat
2. pour new bowl of water
3. feed fish a pinch and sprinkle
4. wake up the blind hamster
5. get hamster from back room
6. give it its daily exercise in ball
(when he's in the ball
he might bump into wall
cat scared of hamster in ball)
7. sometimes give hamster strawberry treats
and whole body will hold treat and nibble it
8. read him a book about hamsters
9. put him back in cage
10. check how he's doing with food and water
11. special key to occasionally get mail
12. put hamster in cage in back room
so cat won't get it and can sleep better
13. occasionally check kitty litter
and take out garbage bags...

Nanook

Who the hell was Nanook of the North? Landlord from Brooklyn
who I used to really like a lot used to always call me Nanook of
the North, but who was he to talk? An out-of-control alcoholic
who every Saturday night like clockwork a whole squad of squad
cars would just show up to their brownstone because of some
brand new drama, which of course he denied because used to
always black-out and then the next day you'd see the whole
holy family parade over for confession, like some procession of
demented Norman Rockwell paintings; his son eternally out
of work working the system for quote on quote disability and
every evening literally hearing him throwing his wife and kid
around sounding like the sound of half-crazed Eskimo madmen in
an igloo of linoleum as all you'd hear is the trail of back and forth
insane echoes; his daughter whose husband got whacked
by La Cosa-Nostra and everytime I showed up to pay the rent
was conveniently wrapped in her towel just coming out of the
shower, asking if I wanted to come in which I really wanted but
didn't want to become the next victim, although in the past had
sincerely gone out with my fair share of Mafia Princesses mostly
from Hell's Kitchen and always touch and go situations; grandson
a dope addict doing inside jobs stealing shit right and left to
support his habit, and myself literally having to drag this old
timer out by his ankles into the hall after he had passed-out
from the heat fixing a leaky faucet in my apartment ranting
and referring to everyone as a hippie and had hair far shorter
than his, but irrelevant as in his reality was convinced, and
honestly found there to be something quite charming even
lovable about him always appearing to slur his words whether
drunk or sober and just seemed to add character to the neigh-
borhood, referring to me as that cat Nanook of the North
I took for something of a sort of backhanded compliment.

Heaven Just A Keen Memory

I wonder if when they bury me
they'll still have me in handcuffs
and will have to wiggle them off
and make a clean break for it
tunneling all the way under
ground to my favorite spot
which was that overgrown
little league sandlot with
ditches and dandelions
where I made a name
for myself and those
old silent home movies
showing me fast-forward
going through the ritual
and routine of banging
my bat a couple times
on the ground before
the pitcher served me one
of his out-of-control wild pitches.
They were always wild back then
and had no control and very proudly
showing me jogging to first base like
some Hollywood hero coming out
of the plane waving or making that
brilliant shoestring catch when that
ball flew right over my shoulder
and turned around on it backwards
like good ol' Willie Mays saving the day
all jumping on top of me at second base
while saving enough room for later on at
Friendly's for a triple scoop with sprinkles.

A.M. Radio

1

i remember writing 1970 with a #2 pencil
(always obsessed that it had to be a #2
and why not a #1 or #3?) on the top right
corner of my composition paper with the
sky-blue thin lines used to balance and
keep straight and in place our words
on the latitude and that 1 long thin red
line on the left longitude to keep it all
in the margin back in 1st grade and this
simple image of me writing 1970 on the
top right corner with my #2 pencil meant
the world i mean was like heaven to me

2

with a whole chorus of cat-call birds
cooing back and forth in perfect rhythmic
echoes, the spirit of these subliminal invisible
creatures we just took for granted and got used
to as long as we knew; weird whirring of big strong
sicilians pushing their mowers in the familiar distance
could not quite put our finger on it when cutting grass
was truly an art form or labor of love and put bread on
the table and the wild white whooshing of great big jumbo
jetliners way up there in the strange and surreal suburban sky

3

when skywriting was big 50/50
chance they were gonna make it
like the big red machine or bronx
bombers winning the world series
and the busy blissful symphony
of all of these things streaming

together without even realizing
it became the soundtrack of our
senses childhood consciousness
or the sum of our memories our
sentimental true-blue existence

4

while in puberty that is when rumors began
and all the shit went down hill from there
like a.m. radio disappearing into thin air.

On The Secretive (Not So Secret) Symbolism Of Soulmates

Married 15 years and still having fantasies
and those erotic dreams of that gorgeous
intellectual girl i used to have long deep
stimulating conversations with in the
cafeteria at yeshiva about foreign
romantic movies the one with ethan
hawke and julie delpy, as she'd tell
the girl i was seeing at the time 'i hope
you didn't think i was flirting...' which
subtly, subliminally, psychologically
really was and just covering herself
(the natural instinct and configuration
of language and defense-mechanisms)
and was so nice and good and pretty and
engaging and in the dream she coyly drops
a photo of herself out of her pocketbook and
i give it back to her and we just start naturally
doing it right there on the floor and i actually
do so with her whole posse as feel obligated
and maybe a bit of my reputation at the time
and think i'm being set up but at that point
don't pay it any mind and in a concretely
sexual way feel this dream represents
getting closure over constant episodes
and feelings of guilt and anxiety and empty
phases with feeling the need to never let
anyone down and always want to please

Wake up with the world off my shoulders...

```
     The Original Madame Tussaud

i see the weather woman
       as something
            of a
    pragmatic porn star
                 giving us
             the ins & outs
                  of the weather
         like some ol' time
                lounge singer
                    who plays
      the exact same
                love songs
                  at the exact same bar
                        night in & night out
in that forgotten
           but romantic
                   hotel
                       down in
           key biscayne,
                   florida
of divorcees
     & debutantes
              & losers
                  & lost souls
                        dead to the world
            claiming they have found god
                     with drinking problems
                washed-up
                        along shore...
```

Right Around The Break Up

How the dewy misty morning smells
like the art shack from summer camp
where you used to mold and shape on
sweltering summer days all that wet clay
to make sculptures and all those artifacts
on the potter's wheel (everything which
miraculously materialized out of the kiln)
and when you went back a couple decades
later after it shut down all mysterious and
overgrown and snuck in there didn't find
anything like love letters and photos
but under all those leaves and stones
and seasons grown old after wiping
the dust off, a musty mildewy copy
of the beatle's *white album* now
of an off-white, a bit discolored
and faded which in many ways
was our own secret treasure
some fragile fossil of nostalgia
or hidden gem from an excavation
which instantly allowed us to piece
everything together and told all
the spirits of love lost, gossip
and rumors turned to gold
the suicides and the soul
looking forward like a bunch
of eager soulful grave robbers
to transport it in stationwagon
back to the suburbs, dust it off
and gently lower it on the turntable
to once more uncover and discover
(no need to play it backwards) how
in fact paul was not dead but tragically
john lennon and everything which had
been so passionately fought for
and meant so much back then.

A Forgotten Amerika

drop-dead vagabond with her wild flowing hair
and quilted sundress gardens across the road

the tied-up canoes from the boy's group home drift
by both just as disoriented and down-in-the-dumps

they wait all day on line at that truck stop
just outside detroit for potato salad like

alice b. toklas got
nothing on them.

Somewhere Between Fate & Mortality

all of life & existence
stems from a single
simple moment
& dream
& fantasy
from child
hood in the 1970's
through your backyard
window romantically
brooding about your
future & tell you
nothing much has
changed when
removing all
the calluses
& scar tissue
exposing that
constantly beating
& palpitating
heart & soul
boogying with
your white boy
afro the king
of bar-mitzvahs.

```
The Secret Life Of Skywriters
```

It's interesting when we first moved to this home
discovered the husband used to be a charter member
of the n.r.a. and would get all of his leftover subscriptions
bullet shells and beer cans scattered all over the backyard
the wife of course i guess supposedly representing some
sort of angel of sorts had all these signs conveniently
planted in the garden with blessings on them while
found the kid's playboy's neatly stashed and hidden
up in the barn turns out of course just like everything
else were moving out due to another divorce and felt
very much like the natural course of events and classic
lack of communication and dysfunction and bullshit
history of "might over right" god bless america.

Wouldn't Wish On My Worst Enemy

Why whenever you run into relatives or old friends
you used to play with and once really enjoyed their
companionship end up disappointed while just like
everybody else like some fucked-up poster child
for adults like those schmuck grownups with those
mean and stingy expressions at funerals, persnickety,
passive-aggressive, paranoid about their cut of
the will; at some casual brunch or get together
constantly looking down at their beeper or
cellphones like they're on-call (and want to
be somewhere else yet really didn't want them
there in the first place) and are engineers who
never even passed the test or psychiatrists who
drive their wives crazy and couldn't put up with
them or trust them and end up divorcing them
and you're wondering when these very self-involved
and self-important self-made something or another's
who play the role of successes will finally just leave
your home and will think twice in the future
about trying to fill in all those empty holes.

```
The Olive Garden
```

Success is a lot like failure only you get the honor
of attending the required annual luncheon at the ceo
of the mental health clinic's country club where that
bullshit supervisor who literally doesn't show up for
supervision (whose purpose is to provide support and
guidance and validation) accepts plaques and awards
at the podium all tearful pretending to be all down to
earth and modest and humble and when you retire
throw that token party for you at your local *olive
garden* where when you're here or there or what
ever the hell they call it get treated like family.

Land Of The Free

He sexts her
& she sexts
him back.
one is a banker
& the other an accountant
guess their own system
of checks & balances.
you wonder in scenarios
like this what exactly
cheating would
look like?

Something Like Faith

In the way up high
mountains of vermont
all i listen to is broken
down staticky symphonies
the only thing which seems
to get through to me and
keeps me going hearing
a very meek seductive
cocktease telling me
something about
being composed
in 1903 by someone
sounding like joe hobo
(wondering if related
to hobo joe) which
to me really doesn't
matter so much at all
as completely apropos
when i flick on the kitchen
radio with all that static
and violins and cellos
at sunup and sundown
barely getting through
and barely getting on
somewhere around
1903 by this bum
named joe hobo

All rivers meet
in the back of
the dairy cream.

Global Warming

All the trees
are dying
in front
of the clap
board home
with all the
windows
open on
the avenue
i hate those
spoiled rotten
liberals almost
as much as i
hate tourists
& alpha-males
white trash
don't know
how lucky
they are
still living
with their
moms
never
leaving
the town
always
with a
convenient
12 pack
of *schlitz* or
old milwaukee
all the gorgeous
ballerinas in their
cut-off shorts come
out of the forest
smiling &
flirtatious
madmen
abound

bringing
character
to the town
the woman
with an opiate
problem decides
to gradually come
out camouflaged
in the hanging
plants of her
overgrown porch
a perfect day
for chinese
buffet on
the river
to lose
yourself
& not
make
a name
for
your
self
i hope my
wife keeps
my number
in her cell
phone after
i bite the dust
like the muenster
cheese she steals
every weekend
from her
group
home.

Just Off Walden

At the place where you
can rent out campers
on the main drag
which runs through
town the sign reads
"prices dropping"
as it's become winter
and colder and snow
falling in a wasteland
of a suburb up on top
of the mountain and love
that idea and bleak image
prefer it so much more
than the idiot *whored*
of summer tourists
hooking up wherever
the fuck idiot tourists
hook up just parking
myself along the side
of some sidling highway
with unmade queen-size
bed and tv and whiskey
perhaps chase it with
a thick holy *mcdonald's*
chocolate shake maybe
some road somewhere
along some abandoned
lake "the ultimate escape"
shooting up dope alongside
walden pond and finally
finding a couple ways
to cope a couple good
dreams couple good nods
nodding off nodding
away nodding-out
in this real-life night
mare of an existence
couple good thoughts
like one day one night

owning my own ram
shackle victorian
under the stars
an overgrown
rambling yard
cats who bark
and dogs who
meow where you
can't ever be bothered
(from what i heard even
the women little crazy
out here and when their
husbands finally take off
to the woods during the
hunting season hang out
in the bars somewhere
around the mountain
to make themselves
available) your camper
camped in the deep
dark forest of fragile
and foreign folklore
besides some babbling
brook being left completely
the fuck alone by this awful
fucken lot of human clones
who just make you feel
so damn alone maybe
a visit every so often
by some massive
gentle giant of a bear
moose rapping very
politely at my door
and leave them
couple of mugs
of some of my
very fine cheap
and leftover merlot
writing love postcards
to old long-lost lovers
and one-night stands

summer romances
which proved to be
just as substantial
as any other mature
relationship in the hopes
to get closure or be a glutton
and start things all up again
against my better judgment
as never thought much about
the very affected and overrated
ethic of judgment (fucked-up
judges and authority figures)
all those fake mother
fuckers so much more
full of hypocrisies
and contradictions
to the point of
being criminal
while always got
so much more true
meaning and wisdom
from instinct and intuition
as well as all things dealing
with impulses and emotion

Prices are falling
and i'm following
from a safe distance.

Whore Frost

I went to *walmart* to pick up some bullshit for the lawn
'cuz it was that time of year and was feeling so lowdown
picked up not only a sprinkler but a whole white trash family
which included this miserable morbidly-obese single mom
who of course hated men; her dirty and filthy kids who ran
back and forth all day long through the sprinkler over our lawn
and experienced this strange phenomenon where they seemed
to get dirtier and dirtier by the second then planted my magical
seeds of squash and sunflowers and even offered this morbidly
obese single mom a wine cooler who of course when i dropped
her off never once thought to thank me or have one nice or kind
thing to say mumbling under her breath but interestingly her kids
as charming as can be (usually the way these things end up going)
and out of the clear blue sky just naturally thanked me as i instantly
reflected back to my childhood with a keen and abundant amount
of fondness and sentimentality as really just the little details in life

When i got home i finished off the wine coolers and caught
the scores and realized this was about as content as i would
ever get and almost zen-buddhist was a real fine feeling at that.

Where I Live

There is a blue house on the corner
which looks over a bridge which
crosses a river and every so
often high school kids after
a full day's labor will strip off
clothing and just leap right in

some showing off
doing somersaults
and back flips
but if not now
then when then
fumbling for their
clothing, slipping
them back on again

full of spirit, disheveled,
sopping wet, picking up
their books and sprinting
home, while could any
childhood scene be
more liberating
and holy?

just the other day a girl got
reported because supposedly
she took off her shirt and dived
in topless; apparently the father's
got two children and only wants
them to be known for procreation.

in my opinion that is totally
ridiculous, prudish, and tasteless
and dream of living in that blue house
on the corner which looks over
the bridge that crosses the river.

Downtime

A bird sits on the wire
brooding, contemplating
silhouetted against the
shuddering horizon feeling
out for the winds, the vibes
before all the rain arrives
just like all those madmen
& drugdealers & hustlers &
runaways & freaks & tomboys
used to run & hide taking shelter
on the stage in tompkins square
park of alphabet city in the lower
east side right when all those torrents
of rain suddenly like a miracle came
crashing down to rid us all of all those
things which made us feel cursed by life
by all the craziness & crises & catastrophes
& always got to know each other so much better
& got so much better acquainted, naturally chatty
curious & gregarious, extroverted, often euphoric
even hysterical, taking great pleasure & interest
in each other's existence, like some grand ball
at the asylum but far more well-mannered
than most formal masquerade parties.

Breakfast Of Champions

A-

Get an e-mail from the wife
and just reads in the subject line
"there's a chicken in the oven
can you take it out" you some
how find yourself amused by
the simple stark image of it all
and what got you to this exact
moment and place and phase in
your existence while can be some
whole other reality or life or time
or past girlfriend (and would that
really make much of a difference?)
or can just answer too in that real
annoying and sarcastic rhetorical
way–i don't know can i? which
ironically actually seems the
most accurate and honest.

B-

Has a suicide note ever been left
with something to remember you by like
one of those deeply pungent melancholic
southern smelling flowers that penetrates
the senses and you can't get rid of how
ever hard you try such as crepe-myrtle
or magnolia; a nice gift certificate to
remember you by such as to *kohl's*
or a couple to *dunkin donuts* to help
your loved one get her through the
summer; a fruit of the month
or book of the month club?

C-

What it all comes down to
in the long-run is you just
want to be left alone like
some swamp or lagoon
ancient, pristine, hissing
vibrant and alive, treasuring
the seasons and passing of time.

Paradise In 6 Easy Installments

1,

Suburbia is never quite cracked
up to what's it's supposed to be
cracked up to be supposed to be
rarely ever really quite real which is
what gives it all it's charm and sex appeal
living happily ever after; deal of a lifetime...
and guess can be just fine but for the most part not
right why throughout our life-cycle we order things
from the back of cereal boxes, catalogues, *marvel* comics
i.e. charles atlas so we won't get picked on or made fun of
and now able to pick up all the girls in their bikini-clad bods
with those x-ray glasses that can see through clothes straight
to the bone of all those milf moms; those seahorses poured
straight from the packet who become a lifelong companion
and grow and develop and come to life right before our eyes
while when you grow up and become profoundly more lonelier
drunken with your clicker somewhere in the wee hours pick
out your favorite color of ring from the tv which is made up
of 100% genuine topaz and gem stone sent straight to your
door at your own convenience as a substitute and far better
version of any man along with a vita-mixer and the latest
state of the art vacuum cleaner whose sleek design
allows you to get into the filthy grime of life in a far
more efficient manner and rapidly clean everything
up lickety-split in one fell swoop and get you
closer to god whenever you might feel uptight
or neurotic while a little later on in those golden
years when mortality creeps in and you are
all alone finishing off a vanilla cake for
the grandchildren fulfilling your quota
of slipping on the linoleum right below
that kitchen counter able to press once
more one of those zapping–'fallen
and i can't get up' buttons which will
alert and bring back together a reunion
of those immortal superheroes in a flash

and drop of the mask straight to your door
to complete that fictional suburban life-cycle
or the hyperbole and caricature and real-life
commercial of some 100 % satisfied final call

2,

You wonder if heaven will be
like one of those farm-o-suedo
commercials with no side effects
where they're blissfully romantically
strolling through some fair or garden
or along some ocean what middle-aged
couples apparently love to do while
eternity will be endless prime rib

3,

Every sunday morning it was "tarzan"
and "abbot & costello" and looking
back could anything have been more
elevated, liberating, and sentimental?

4,

Shortcuts, delicate, fragile, secretive and sacred
translucent, verdant, iridescent, laden with angels
and delinquents, declaring their love for each other
romantic and reflective, time immemorial, transcendent
with moments which seemed to last forever, tinctured
with dappled pools of palpable sun and tender multi-
color leaves of scarlet and golden dripping in the bright-
eyed breeze of breathing autumn, mercurial in the magical
hush of the whisper and gusts of introspective seasons
singing, disappearing within the solitary stir of spirits
not caring a wink when you reached your destination

5,

Growing up in new york you went out with mafia princesses,
cuban bombshells, the daughters of korean diplomats to die for,
girls whose fathers were the cult leaders of the moonies with
security always ominously perched on the roof of very posh
private schools, jewish girls with borderline disorder and such
insecure identities who never could live up to the unrealistic
expectations of overbearing domineering parents left feeling
eternally empty and guilty, constantly in between something
suicidal or blaming you for all their problems as this to me is
what true diversity was all about, trying to survive and cope
and save others when you couldn't even save yourself while at
summer camp or trips to ski slopes where they always came back
either drug addicts (former ghosts of themselves) or no longer
virgins (promiscuous coke whores) pretending like they never
knew you, now mandated to see a Freudian after feeling so
damn lonely and they stole everything from you (including your
innocence and all previous, apparent truths) from connections
from other opportunistic manipulative parents who similarly,
ironically, completely brainwashed and seemed to screw...

6,

Today my wife and son and i went out to a roadside stand
in the drizzle to get a couple of burgers which triggered
me to this facebook photo of some old friend of mine
from childhood who i hooked up with just recently
and just knew after chatting for a little while it
could only last for so long and actually did go
a bit longer than expected; him being like every
male on the face of the planet just talking about
his family and kids and existence but the pattern
as always with the male of the species being
self-centered and incomplete, never asking
any questions about me (every man in reality
is 'an island unto himself' his own self-made
megalomaniac trying to "steal" his wealth).
he moved out to some 'exclusive' suburb in
pennsylvania and had a pool and 2 daughters

and a wife who was a lawyer and eventually
changed that photo which he had up for like
months on end; what i guess he thought made
him look handsome or what he believed represented
what it was to be content in his tank top and health
club muscles and had a sleazy coy smile with a beer
in a brown paper bag after they had just got off
one of those miserable cruises, and to me that
simple image seemed to just sum up everything
about the absurdity and superficiality and pettiness
of reality, even our time here on earth; moving to
the suburbs going on one of those cruises, pretending
you're not miserable with a wife and 2 children still nursing
that beer out of a brown paper bag trying to convince others.

Suicide Tries Really A Desperate Stab At Life

All those crazy loves
        we were gonna
try to rescue ourselves
move to one of those
high-rise condos
in the upper east
side
in no
mans
land
in man
hattan
right a
round
that tram
which went
no where
& never
saw the
nomads
to that
sci-fi
island
no one
knew
what
they
did
one just simply
disappeared
in the mist
of bellevue
& back to
the life with
her mad
brothers
in the
irish mob
& the other

a highly
intel
gent
jew
ish
girl
used to
speak fluent
russian from
riverdale
where archie
& veronica
hailed from
& a damn
swell part
of the bronx
while what life
did to her really
never had a chance
yet looking back
at all that needy
desperate romance
learned to never take
a damn thing for granted.

Where The Wounds Begin

the best education
at that idiot southern
school were the brothers
across the hall having
one hell of a good time
on the football team
from the inner city
of l.a. & used
to hang out with
them with sizzling
burgers on their
mini grills passing
around the blunt
& *white rose*
& was able
to relate
to them so
much more
than those
mean-spirited
rich privileged
entitled jewish
kids from the
tri-state area
coming down
in the cars
their parents
purchased
for them with
personalized
license plates
& were so cruel
& alienating
when all you
could do was
turn to long
bicycle rides
chasing the
streetcar down

st. charles & that
impenetrable scent
of magnolia which
stuck to you forever
to the cobblestone
& ghosts & phantoms
of the french quarter
contemplating &
taking in the spirits
of the mississippi
until you felt like
enough of them
rubbed off you
& returned home
at sunset feeling
cursed & blessed
where the wounds
got their start &
began to open.

The Cost Of Living

the stenographer
just sits there
in her empty chair
staring straight ahead
waiting for the whole
cast to show up
the prosecutors
& defense attorney
& the judge
& witnesses
she just sits there
in her empty chair
& stares straight ahead
& waits for all
the gross detail
of man with really
bad judgment
& poor character
all the sleazy
& see-through
histrionics of
the lawyers
like awful
unconvincing
actors making
deals having
absolutely nothing
to do with the issue
at hand & law of the land
the stenographer just sits
there in her empty chair
& stares straight ahead
at the judge up there
high up there
on his high
horse acting
like the whole
world revolves
around him

trying to stare
everyone
down
looking
to put (down)
the fear of god
into all these
peasants
in his
false
self-
absorbed
kingdom
the stenographer
just sits there
in her empty
chair & stares
straight ahead
the witnesses
who appear just
as guilty as the one
being accused due
to their herd-mentality
& going in for the kill
the stenographer just
sits there in her empty
chair & stares
straight ahead
the rest of the court
acting all carefree
& casual like
this is some
sort of ball
or lifestyle
& thrive off it
while thank
the lord
it ain't them
in their lost
& blind
brain-

washed
existence
of closed-
minded
conformist
the stenographer
just sits there
in her empty
chair & stares
straight ahead
she just recently
became single
& has one kid
finding out her
husband was
involved in all
these extra-
marital
affairs
all these
extra-
curricular
activities
in the con
struction
business
the stenographer
just sits there
in her empty
chair & stares
straight ahead
she makes $32/hr
coming straight out
of stenographer school
& part of the union
& not sure who's
paying their dues
the stenographer
just sits there
in her empty chair
& stares straight ahead

she's a damn fine girl
& always been organized
& detail-oriented most
likely overcompensating
from an abusive childhood
as all she ever wanted
was a nice & stable
family & someone
to look up to with a
home to call her own
the stenographer just sits
there in her empty chair
& stares straight ahead
waiting for her life
to finally begin
waiting for all
the gross & vulgar
details hoping to make
life seem a little less
empty & miserable
little more livable
& manageable
searching for someone
anyone who will finally
'tell the truth the whole
truth and nothing
but the truth
indivisible
with liberty
and justice
for all...'

Traveling

when i die
i just want
my wife
to dump
my tired
bones
right on
the porch
none of
that fancy
schmanzy
futile
funeral
nonsense
where every
one goes
around
the room
sharing
their true blue
experiences
& bullshit
stories
& excuses
& andedotes
just wanting
to hear their
own voices
in warhol's
15 minutes
of fame
perhaps
even leave
me with
the house
plants
& cactuses
during
the rainy

season
forgetting
i'm out there
& wondering
what to do
with me
leaving me
all coiled-up
like a bullet
ridden dillinger
or billy the kid
when they're
sweeping
in & out the
screen doors
scraping burgers
off the grill & finally
figure what i really
would have preferred
loading me up in my
duffel bag where i took
all my travels & unravel
& let me go down that river
(perhaps even with some left
over sand & maps & guide books)
which flows past the capitol
& gorgeous ghetto & dairy
cream all the way into
the deep green mountains
up into north country
separates the hudson
& lake champlain
& the adirondacks
& montreal city
& st. lawerence
& quebec city
just take a job where
i can work minimum wage
& get consistent hours
working behind the
postcard carousel

where the pilgrims
in top hat & tails
used to travel.

The United States Of America

This morning my kid was in the dark hall
still in his pajamas, groggy-eyed, but acutely
aware and happened to mention as the day
before in like a hour or so had remembered
every one of the states and all their capitols
(has a weird photographic memory like myself)
"wouldn't it be cool if they made you remember
all the rivers and tributaries as well?" something
which has always been a fixation and fascination
of mine, and responded like every 13 year old
i suppose–"yeah i guess so" and then when he
took off and wandered back down the hall heard
him mutter under his breath–"what's up pussycat?"
i asked him how he knew that and just retorted–
"i just do" and wondered if that had anything to
do with wittgenstein's concept and theory of man
having a predisposition for learning language. i found
myself the rest of the morning for some strange reason
humming biggie's line–"the feds hate me" and wondered
if that had anything subconsciously to do with the line of
"what's up pussycat?" and just turned on the scores from
the night before and thought it would be so damn cool if they
just devoted a full channel to showing all these bucolic scenes
of like covered bridges and farms and trees all covered in dew.

On The Nature Of Porn & Weather

How long did it take the weatherman or what do you call them
these days "weather experts" or meteorologists to come up with
the name of Reynolds Wolf just sounds like some real gung-ho
goal-oriented porn star who's just gonna tell us anyhow about
some brand-new asshole captain being brought up on charges
for abandoning his passengers and capsized cruise ship; how
the flood waters are starting to recede and go down in Texas
just leaving the muckety-muck sediment and stranded jungle
gym; whole new storm brewing around Topeka, North Platte,
Sioux Falls always some new storm brewing around Topeka,
North Platte, and Sioux Falls; those low-flying planes you
thought were either gliders from childhood or sputtering
bi-planes pulling banners over tattoo beach or maybe even
fugitives on-the-run; turns out was the Federal Bureau of
Investigation flying undercover over the ghettos of America
checking out whatever suspicious activity after the riots
as if they haven't seen enough; Delores telling us Dustin's
on his way to fix our electric problem (emotional problems?)
other handymen who all do 'inside jobs' no matter how nice
you are always turn out to be crooks and criminals as detect
and diagnose we got more, but got no idea about your night-
mares and how hard it is for you to roll out of bed so somehow
justify ripping us off and will most likely turn to the bottle
what's even worse don't have an honest bone in the body
(moral fiber?) not like that Reynolds Wolf meteorologist.

Infomercials: one's mortality in modern times

Up in the high
mountains
we choose
our news
by the
weather
women
whether
we are
fond
of large
or small
breasted
big-boned
& buxom
mrs. robinson
or doe-eyed lolita
who we dream
& fantasize of
& their sunny
& rosy glow
& bedside
manner.
they now
got this
radar
from *google*
which starts
way up
in the stars
of heaven
then shoots all
the way down
to track down
down to earth
on the grid
lay of
the land
whether

in the city
or suburbs
the criminals
the meth labs
the church break
ins & will give
their full names
for purposes of
full disclosure
more accurately
the natural
consequences
& humiliation
& stigmatization
3 escaped convicts
& live-action
police lingo
over their
walkie-talkies
showing exactly
which way
down the street
they are heading.
when you wake up
in the middle of the
evening from your disrupted
sleep-cycle from acid-reflux
the television now shows self-
soothing images of diagrams
& anatomies & that very
lean clean-cut english man
with his english accent
(some man/ic mania/c
man/made mad/man)
hollering hysterically
about some holy
all-purpose fluid
which will naturally
remove every stain
known to man
kind as well as

miraculously
heal all
your
doubts
& fears
& guilt
which
has built
up over
the years
& make them
instantly vanish
& disappear
then the weather
which will of course
make everything better
effecting your reality
& moods
& behaviors
practically telling
you everything
you should
be expecting
dry in the high's...
then some perfect
svelte wife with
her bright eyes
& natural wide
madonna/whore
ivory girl smile
& convenient
vacuum with all
its attachments
& accoutrements
& ammunition
for the suburbs
& like some
graceful ballerina
runs & maneuvers
over the safe & secure
comforts & problem

contained area
of the living room
the wall to wall carpet
the sofas the curtains
even shows her hitting
the lampshade while in
one fell swoop humorously
getting the shaggy dog
who is just hanging
out there minding
his own business
while this fleeting
long-lasting image
of her who may
also be viewed
as something
of a possession
allows you to
sleep and live
happily ever after.

```
Ready Or Not
```

Has war now all just become some brilliant satire come to life?
The Russians now doing airstrikes and taking-out innocent
civilians of rebel-backed forces? America doing airstrikes
and taking-out innocent civilians of Assad-backed forces?
(Like some insane ridiculous version of musical chairs)
So I guess the winner is just the literal last man (woman
and child) standing, as suppose that cliché really does
hold true; we're all just a sum of our parts (and losses)

Missing those good ol' nostalgic days where
by mistake used to bomb aspirin factories–

"Soldier Asked To Step Outside Waffle House..."

Getting Ready For The Upcoming Mosquito Season

The weather woman in her leopard print dress
and madonna/whore complex sweeps her hand
over the upper midwest and for memorial day
weekend tells us about budgets on the strip.
pfizer finally decides to stop selling their
knock-out potion to penitentiaries for
prisoners strapped down on death row
while local news tells us a racetrack
was broken into, mailboxes destroyed
from a drunken driver along with
his glossy photo and a close-up
of 5 prom queens in their sequins
with great big elastic smiles looking
like they're about to swallow you up.
you think you need a vacation to one
of those budget hotels she was talking
about then go on to report the results
and statistics of those circus lions
when they're let back in the wild.

Your Love Boat Crew

1,

Stowaway can never seem to find his way
and runs into all the old shriners in the lobby
on bowling night. their wives are the true history
buffs in the family and clap their hands in a plume
of chalk dust as civilization starts up. the front desk
clerk knows all their dreams but can't say anything
as considered in the vein of insider trading. the very
sophisticated ladies bend over to sneak peeks through
the keyholes at their fantasies or a life which has passed
them by then go back to playing the role of socialites and
ignoring everyone. they're all whining which helps time
go by quicker. every new day a pennypincher is born

2,

The weather will be a burnt down rollercoaster...

3,

What happened to all those bands who did those power ballads?
my mother refused to let me see styx in concert on a school
night and could never understand shit like that and still can't
(like discipline or deprivation all for the sake of something
draconian and dickensian) and think i would have become
such a more cultured well-rounded man something you
can't find at the met or whitney or gugghenheim museum

Shit, looking back they even turned away basquiat!

4,

The wildlife of home movies...

5,

The statistics for sons of clinical narcissists
suicide ideations, self-fulfilling prophecies,
self-destructive behavior, and if get lucky
survive like those seahorses who never
quite came to life all stemming from a
self-loathing very weak fragile identity

6,

I'm going to invent a new therapy
for when marriages start to become
stale or too domestic or constant
power-struggles and can meet up
with girls from high school you used
to have crushes on or mad girlfriends
you never got closure and plant one
last fantastic kiss beneath some
tenebrous bridge at dusk or way
a'top a glittering skyscraper
in the brilliant anonymous
maddening muffled hush

7,

That black girl i used to date
and met under the bridge in the rain
told me she knew when things got
really out of hand when drug dealers
got mortgages and moved next door

she grew up in yonkers and her dad
was blind and hard-working and ended
up owning a whole string of bodegas

wonder what ever became of her
and always came over when
i had no one to turn to

8,

Why after one of those daily massacres in america
do they always show pictures like on the computer
of one of those perfectly-sculpted gi joe characters
with their rifles and armor as wouldn't it have been
better and more effective if they had showed up
before as opposed to after? our katharine hepburns
and marilyn monroes taking nude selfies in the bathroom

9,
..
Child stars who have the need to break
out of their roles and literally break
the mold every chance they get
take off their clothes and then
when they get older very
sincerely and sentimentally
do commercials for abused
animals and starving
children in africa

10,

If during the slave trade they had infomercials
tv would have read something like–"free shipping"

11,

Every day adds to my ptsd

12,

Like charlie chaplin the tramp
being rescued by bruce lee

13,

Being dragged off
to the horizon
with his cane
and pained
smile...

Situational Depression

So our tv tells
us about tensions
conflict, violence
in the middle east
which includes
real-life beheadings,
stabbings, stonings,
suicide bombings
"and the beat goes on"
while in america when
it starts to turn to fall
(something they consider
in the category and genre
of 'the holiday season')
they show gung-ho boys
in their fantasy world
in artificial jungles
with their brave
and courageous
g.i. joes pushing
tonka trucks
and *lego's*
saving the world
half-crazed girls
whipping out their
pastel state-of-the-art
transitional-object dolls
where they can
brush their hair
burp them and
start to take
control, as
their parents
have all become
convenient parables
for psychotropic
medication
and some
sort of newly

made-up disease
and symptoms
with side effects
which prove to be
more lengthy and lethal
than the original prognosis
and forget about the med
which is supposed to heal
them where they suddenly
become fluent and proficient
and their own spokesperson

Your eyes are burning
and probably got one of
those tension-fatigue syndromes.

Might Call This A Might Over Right Manifesto

bullet point: we now have a tyrant who has had his
token temper-tantrum & threatened with blackmail
& a real-life ultimatum presently holding the country
hostage because they would not give him his funds to
build his silly little sci-fi wall & shut down the government

bullet point: we have a thief who threw his hat in the ring
& developed his reputation just like mccarthey based on
false accusations & conspiracy & demagoguery, racist
innuendo & implications that our first black president
was not born in this country & thus did not earn
the honor & respect (the personification of
emotional neglect) of his title & standing

bullet point: we have this higher-than-holy, soulless hotelier
who made his millions by bilking the public off trump wine,
trump airlines, trump university & trump enterprises, declared
bankruptcy multiple times & still not paid back a majority of the
contractors (& all those "illegals") who helped build his quasi-empire

bullet point: we have some schmuck who after the central park 5
through d.n.a. testing were found innocent & cleared of all crimes
(saw jail time) opined that we should still give them the death penalty

bullet point: we have some freak who announced his candidacy
coming down the gold-gilded escalator of his corrupt criminal
kingdom based on the notion that all mexicans
are gang members & rapists & drug dealers

bullet point: we have some reality show/belligerent barker
who tries to brainwash us (on the deal & delusion) to keep
our borders safe & secure keeps children locked up in cages
& meeting the criteria & all the symptoms of clinical narcissism
pulls out of all necessary agreed-upon international treaties, denies
global warming, mass shootings & has no problem sleeping
with all of these other forms of genocide & atrocities

bullet point: we have some ventriloquist/dummy falsely claim
with his tally of future 5,550 recorded lies growing by the day

that when the world trade center went down he actually saw
crowds of palestinians dancing wildly in the streets of jersey

bullet point: we have some punk who boasted how he could
shoot someone right in the middle of 5th avenue & would
face absolutely no consequences & get away with it

bullet point: we have a commander-in-chief complete control freak
who absurdly has tried to not only manipulate all systems of
democracy & free speech but even history where the stocks
have dropped & plummeted to an all-time low on christmas
eve which has not been seen since the great depression

bullet point: so in conclusion when we speak about kings & tyrants
isn't this exactly what we were warned about & what the revolutionary
war & civil war & world war II & the declaration of independence &
emancipation proclamation & constitution all represented & fought for?

bullet point: so i implore you what does it finally take & how much
do we have to be pushed & played (& betrayed) where is that one
single sincere brave soul & man of courage & honesty & integrity
who is not afraid & a slave to politics & their constituency & maybe
even be like one of those real-life statesmen or forefathers from back
in the day of individuality & independent thinking & willing to actually
serve & sacrifice themselves for the good of the country & stand up
to this see-through blatant & obvious abuse of power tyranny?

bullet point: chuck d. of the infamous rap group public enemy
poetically politically poignantly declared–"if you don't
stand up for something you'll fall for everything."

Post-Trauma

i pray hopefully our next body
of government is run by just
blonde women with mad spirit
as just so much more positive &
productive & connect & function
so much better when doing the weather
the next morning the day after thanksgiving
giving us warnings out in eureka & reno
& portland, oregon; chicago, jackson
hole, wyoming, that whole swathe
between the great lakes & vermont
the bible belt which includes charlotte
& savannah & antebellum islands off
of georgia & somehow begin to try
& heal all the damage done by this
fucked-up madman president with
our long-standing european allies

redemption doesn't come that easy
but maybe it just does & hopefully
they know in most ways we had
absolutely nothing to do with it

how does that stones song
go again–"it's sure been
a long cold winter…"

in the morning eat
leftover apple pie
& red wine

& spend the rest
of the day with
jimmy stewart
& james cagney

when black & white
seemed just a little
less complicated &
helped us to get by.

```
On The Hx Of Real Estate
```

You start to think doesn't d. trump
resemble and look a lot like that white
devil with his long hunting rifle and safari
hat soulless sociopathic knowing and
feeling he's always about to do some
really crazy shit without conscious
sheisty and illegal when you used
to eagerly watch *tarzan of the jungle*
each and every sunday morning and
couldn't wait till you saw and heard
tarzan suddenly swing in from the top
of the miraculous majestic trees yodeling
madly mellifluously from the top of his lungs

Well i ask you america where the hell's
our super hero to come in and save the day
as isn't this why they were originally created?

Ventriloquist Found Guilty In Murder/Suicide

In america
what it means
to be completely
content to reach
that highest state
of self-actualization
and nirvana is jogging
working-out something
aerobic money back if not
fully satisfied money back
if not fully satisfied money
back if not fully satisfied
and left nodding-out
somewhere in the deep
dark night early morning
after a bout of insomnia
if you really need that
vita-mix or vegetable
slicer or knife sharpener
while still can't find just that
one girl to make things right
to trust and believe in and make
your life seem worthwhile working
your ass off just to try and make ends
meet and pay your rent to that landlord
still refusing to give you heat for the winter

which ironically has
everything to do with
shipping and handling.

For Armageddon...

The blonde-haired cheerleaders are all shipped-in
not the ones on academic scholarship but the sluts
from the sororities doing close-ups of million-dollar
smiles shaking their luscious ta-ta's and silver metallic
pompoms in front of the cameras; the middle-aged
pasty-faced coach has already pulled out all the hair
from his scalp due to the diagnostic statistic manual
for personality disorders called "trichotillomania"
as all the wealthy white boy wiggers from the suburbs
try to look all intimidating and threatening from a safe
distance in their herd-mentality as phenomenologically
or process of elimination that great big exploding ball
of fire never gets noticed in the distance, all brought
to you by Gatorade and "Black Mass" the Whitey Bulger
story, based on one of the biggest mass-murderers known
in American Hx–"Johnny Depp gives a breathtaking..."

An In-Depth Didactic Case Study Of C. Stooge

Hole half-baked cookie-cutter culture
society where everybody's taking
selfies all seeming so excited and
satisfied and contented like some
affected made-up spontaneity?
From the pope to the president
to what? Prisoners on death row?
I prefer way back in the day when
Curly all decked-out at the bougy
ball looked sincerely straight into
the camera or flower stuck to some
bigwig lapel and the water suddenly
squirted straight-out at him and lost
it caught him smack-dab lickety-split
right in the middle of the ol' punim
which I swear on my mother's eyes
with all his fear and frustration seemed
to sum-up and encompass the whole range
of emotions and mean so much more than
all of false society and culture put together.

On The Origins Of Kojak Or The Nature Of First Love

What happened to Telly Savalas with that rough and tough
quick thick New York accent suavely sucking on his lollipop
right in the middle of the filthy and grimy police precinct?
I think our problem these days is that we have no real
Telly Savalas to believe in or rely on or save the day.
I remember when we were kids going on vacation
I think somewhere down in Key Biscayne, Florida
borrowing our aunt's condo where I fell in love
with my first love at ten-years old from the same
neighborhood (and when we got home went on our
first date to see the movie *Rocky*) and there was this
same lounge singer night in and night out repeatedly
playing "Piano Man" over and over again from Billy Joel's
first or second album (while I guess having to do with the concept
of object-permanence or just always 'being there' felt sentimental)
and over the previous day had seen Telly Savalas out of nowhere
simply lounging around the pool in some fur coat in the sweltering
weather reading his script for an upcoming "Kojak" episode and
was like that's one strange crazy dude (might have even thought
what drug are you on?) even took really bad pictures from afar
yet at that moment life somehow did seem to sincerely mean
a little more even though the pictures didn't turn out so well
nor for that matter the relationship with that ten-year old girl.

Twin Portraits

I.

If you turn on the tv these days
america seems fixated, depraved,
half-crazed, pathetically priding itself

on sadistic & satanic
& can't get away from
their techno contraptions.

america should be run
by that pretty red head girl
from those car commercials

& swear should just drop her
like a bomb; this pretty alabaster
red-haired goddess to (live &) die for

in her blue jeans & flannel
& subtle seductive smile
long flowing blazing red

hair lighting the place on fire
which in my opinion would be
the cure to all the world's problems.

II.

Demure, shy & self-conscious.
she straps back on her bra
like the back of a fragile

delicate guitar in the dark
& we fall into slumber
in that secret motel

on the silhouetted ocean
of echoes & swells.
you may call this

a one-night stand
even a final stand
but something that

will remain forever
as long as it will last
even guess might say

she is "the bomb" or an angel
who has suffered & seen way
too much capable of imploding

any time or any moment
from a literal hair-trigger
from abusive relationships

from bad luck
or just poor
choices.

any which way you slice it
she remains forever etched
in your consciousness

this beautiful blazing
red head who lives
just out of town

forgotten on the river
where all the mills
burned down.

comes in all different
shapes & sizes
which includes

the mind body
heart & soul
& spirit

like some
incandescent beacon
in the darkening season.

Reservation Not Required

If i could i would own a boxcar diner that just sold
grilled cheese & bacon & hashbrowns getting better
by the second, stored up on top of the oily grill.
the only people admitted would be young lovers
and old timers who were romantics and in it for
the long haul. the waiters and waitresses would
be all those turned-out by their family with nowhere
else to go. the cooks, crooks and criminals and former
acrobats who walk with long-term limps from the circus.
the owner, who responsibly takes painkiller cuz he's got
pain killer! the pictures on the wall would just be made up
of jigsaw puzzles with missing pieces, and would not be able
to read or aloofly, obnoxiously snap any one of those papers
and the only thing made available would be *the saturday
evening post* and *national geographic*; the short stories of
tolstoy and doestoevsky and turgenev, ernest hemingway
and sherwood anderson; for dessert real apple strudel
from the motherland, washed down by boilermakers
to help the customers get home more safe & secure,
spiritually, sentimentally when reflecting and doing
all of that necessary talk therapy to themselves...

Saints & Hoboes

1

bury me under a paper airplane

2

bury my bones below a paper airplane crashed into a home

3

bury my crushed heart & soul
which has crashed into shattered windows

4

bury it all my mind body spirit & soul beneath a paper airplane
which has made a crash landing on the front lawn

5

bury me ! bury me! and if they say in fact when you die
you see your whole life flash right in front of your eyes
let me be some half-crazed satisfied passenger with a
wise ass smile looking out the windows of that paper
airplane mucking it up with my childhood buddies

6

bury me! bury me! bury me! bury me! to finally figure out
life is just some simple spare paper airplane sailing freely
never quite sure where and when you'll reach your destiny

7

bury my memories
and the rest of it all
below some paper airplane
which never quite took off.

```
Blues: Or One Of Those Shell Games
You Play On The Avenue At Your Funeral
```

When i die i just want them to wrap me up
in one of those ole polynesian table cloths
a mummification ceremony where past erotic
girlfriends just wipe me down with one of those
warm steamy towels and the hearse keeps on
forgetting to bring my broken bones to the dug
out hole until the whole half-witted procession
of cut-throat family members just get fed up
in a postmodern version of the boy who cried
wolf and the only one who shows up is that
pretty little leftover angel from *the dairy cream*
looking sweeter than one of those vanilla
ice creams you get out of the machine.

It was always those rude girls who put-out that i trusted...
never goody-goody prudes always making me feel like nothing.

Land Of Palm Springs

I remember as a teenager
listening to neil young's
country-influenced
brilliant sentimental
ballad "comes a time"
reflective, ruminating
tears in my eyes staring
through the car window
in the middle of the mohave
in the gorgeous majestic
maddening mountains
of palm springs, california
my best friend's parents
taking me on vacation
with them as a buffer
so he wouldn't argue
with his sister, quick
and clever as always
stealing some absurd
irrelevant item (literally
reaching out for help due
to a domineering father)
some *chilly willy* thingamajig
to keep your beer cold from one
of those huge suburban california
supermarkets, his father ironically
being some bigwig lawyer having
firms back in new york and also
out there, while you still having
'a heart of gold' and remember
distinctly seeing billboards
just suddenly show up out
of nowhere in the middle
of the desert protesting
bullfighting not knowing
why back then (guess
just the 'bullshit'
of human nature
and what life deals

or steals from you)
which only found out
until much later on, out of
pure jealousy, completely
turning his back on me
for no reason in particular
something of a custom
and tradition and reality
which happened regularly
in that sort of society and
never once having a mean
bone in my body–"you and
i, we were captured, we
took our souls and we
flew away..." fucken
coward that he was.

Munchausen

After my wife and i got married i tried doing
the whole grownup thing, but just never was
particularly successful at it, inviting colleagues
over from the mental health clinic to garden parties
supervisors, the head of accounting, fellow therapists
with miserable marriages you already knew everything
about from all the gossip in between clients; the other side
of the family which hated them and all their sexual disorders
and ironically complete dysfunction and lack of communication
and guess suppose just never got too good at it or plainly for
that matter, at all really too interested, as just felt or seemed
way too sensationalistic or soulless and not particularly capable
or fluid in pacing myself with how long i should spend with each
individual wife or they felt the need to spend with me or some
husband i had absolutely no interest in meeting and nothing
in common and no real connection (with any of their boring
grownup anti/dose and hobbies) and all the bullshit and
innuendos flying and collective laughter with obvious
and rather passive-aggressive, hostile punch lines
often of a munchausen design which only seemed
to sincerely highlight how pathetic and petty and
empty their existence truly was, and all i could
maybe think of was perhaps spending some time
with a babysitter down the dead end which bordered
the wilderness or just being one of those free-floating
pieces of scooped-out fruit drenched in sangria swimming
solitary at the bottom of some hollowed-out watermelon...

How To Soothe A Savage Beast

Whenever my wife burns
something on the stove
it smells exactly like
those warm chestnuts
on cold frozen winter
nights in hell's kitchen.
i ask her to burn things
more often and tell her
it's great for the soul
homecooking
straight from
the oven...

```
Moon Pie
```

i got gobbled up by a plate of milk and cookies
leaving just my crumbs under the moon and stars.

one wonders if you can get on the good side
of ghosts because trust me have suffered just

as much and get all the pain and anguish
and injustice and routine and ritual of all

the manipulation and brain
wash and bullshit repetition.

Tradition

my wife keeps on getting
disappointed by my
behavior night in &
night out as i call out–
"er-rrica!" & hearing
her sweet voice chime
through the door–
"i'm with dylan joey!"
darting back & forth
between her chores
a bath of bubbles
& getting his bed
ready with apples,
chocolate milk,
a nightlight &
the hardy boys.

```
American Hx
```

this morning she told me–

did i tell you the 5th grade is doing a revolutionary war musical
at the end of april? he has to wear a trenchcoat...black sweat
pants and a strange hat...he's gonna be servant #4...how
do they determine who's gonna be servant #1, 2, and 3?

and you look at her blankly
like most punchlines
at the end of
futile riddles.

The Smell Of Downpour

i remember when my phlebotomist
told me she thought i had beautiful
eyes and didn't feel that very much
inside while starving and donating
my blood and took me back to her
home on her postage stamp lawn
and out of nowhere like they always
do told me her husband was some
bouncer of sorts and then showed
me her bowl of snapping piranhas
which only turned me off more and
made me lose more respect for her
and guess i was supposed to make
the moves on her but just didn't feel
very much like it or in the mood or
for that matter worth it with her idiot
bouncer husband looming somewhere
in the distance and just dropped me off
on the corner in portland, oregon and
spent the rest of the night reading books
camped-out in the aisles like some runaway
scholar constantly underestimated which
only made me that much more motivated
and worth my while and became a solitary
tradition and felt far more satisfying and
made my way back home to my room with
the sink in the corner at *the jack london*
not knowing a living breathing soul and
a panoramic view of the alley and the
seasons changing somewhere in the
secret distant heavenly valley through
all that constant verdant misty rain &
rain & rain & rain which if falls long
and hard enough does wash away
all the pain and don't tell me it
doesn't have a very concrete fleeting
consistent aroma and way of making
you feel starting to put up domestic scenes
in the foreign windows of department stores

for the holidays coming just around the corner
feel-good films at the end of purple-lit elevators.

Living The Life

i was watching
the *good times*
marathon
and john
amos
who played
that head-
strong
hand-
some
father
was just
going
through
his down-
trodden
exercise
of sitting
at the
table
steaming
about to
explode
all down
on his luck
poverty-
stricken
and
fucked-up
for pretty
much all
the right
real-life
reasons
nursing
his beer
and thought
these days
with all

the bull-
shit of
political-
correctness
they'd say
such shit
like "drink
responsibly"
which would
only trigger
and make
me feel
more
isolated
and de-
pressed
and want
to knock
down a
couple
6-packs
in the
chicago-
land
projects
with
john
amos
the father
from good
times
guzzling
a couple
cold ones
irresponsibly–

"Just looking
out of the
window..."

On The Essence Of Light

i remember those
couple times
they put us
in jail how
they took our
shoe laces away
in case we should
ever happen to try
& impulsively hang
ourselves as if those
sarcastic & sadistic
c.o.'s would ever give a shit
threatening to get us when
we got out & gave us a couple
cheeseburgers from *mcdonald's*
& remember feeling really let down
as felt like no thought went into it
& completely mechanical & if i
was going to have to spend a night
in tombs in downtown manhattan
the least they could give us was
bread & butter & when i got out
in the light of morning strolling
through chinatown when they
put the fish out found my
self with a great big smile
(one of those maddening
smiles when you're cursing
to yourself) really appreciating
the wind & sun as if for the first
time ever & what it means to be
a free man when the devils no longer
have the control & power & you're no
longer a statistic or number & invisible
feeling like just experienced all the hell
& bullshit & injustices of nightmare
america & real-life lowlife police
brutality for no reason in particular
still trying to figure & when you

first discover there is no justice
& don't ever get yourself stuck in
the system or you're a dead duck
like one of those dead ducks
hanging from *shanghai joe's*
on hester & straight-up from
the gut right there on the spot
learn & develop the principle
& concept of insight & wisdom
which is perspective & what they
steal from you something i wouldn't wish
on my worst enemy well maybe just a little.

Domestic Violence: a love sonnet

1.

i saw the first mall go up
and saw all the malls shut
which was my later-adolescence
with no one around and felt like
total abandonment. i fell in love
with the voice of dionne warwick
who was all the babysitters i fell in love
with. it seems like i always had my window
open to lush suburban lawns and the cat-calls
of birds and olivia newton-john and think it was
good that i didn't really know what went down
in those neighbors' homes. all the alcoholism.
all the adultery. all the anger. that kid next
door who got the tracheotomy. the insider
trading. the embezzlements. and forgot
about it all zooming my *schwinn* bicycle
with my best friend next door through
the dewy lawns at dawn to carpenter's
pond. shame on any blocking or denial

the sound of lou rawls...

2.

i was the specimen leftover
neglected in the petri dish
the kids forgot to pick up
before flying out the door
like the running of the bulls
to recess but was still always
able to appreciate and never
take for granted the sun slanting
through the filthy blinds of science

3.

how to make baloney & cheese sandwiches in a toaster oven
how to turn the lights off in the middle of the auditorium
how to go flying through a glass door hollering superman
how to fondle her bosom with your arm around her shoulder
still bullshitting with your buddies intoxicated at a house party

4.

i think i'm just like my mother
and hate lights on in the morning.
i always seem to have a pack
of matches in my pants during
the winter in case i have to light
candles. i love looking at the mirror
through the bathroom window at the
heap of mountains in the back of the
house for that moose they're always
telling me about and just the exercise
and the image of never seeing him
around but knowing he's somewhere
out there somehow means the world

5.

your kid in his bruce lee
hugh hefner bathrobe
with his big puff of
dirty-blonde hair
eats his waffle
at the kitchen island
very casually while completely
focused and reading his graphic
novels and of course his mini
storm troopers keeping him
company keeping an eye out
on the surrounding area

6.

i can't stand those couples
who always seem to find each other
on those irritating on-line dating commercials
and feel the compulsion to always tell us
about their life story as if we're supposed
to give a shit and be all happy for them
and don't make much of a distinction
or seem like the exact same assholes
only a little older all privileged and entitled
in those erectile dysfunction commercials
america's version of growth & development

7.

wife tells me the bug guy
is coming today at 11:00.
i tell her you better not have
an affair with the bug guy.
just think how you'll feel.
she tells me he's a douche
and turns on her blow dryer.
i tell her to please turn the lights
off. they're driving me crazy. she tells me
it's not *burger king* and can't have it my way

8.

later on i am just looking out my winter window
and see this runaway girl walking along the side
of the road not sure if she is a runaway but
sure as heck seemed so; her emotion and
her passion and following her every move
and motion and think she might have even
been friends with the girl next door not sure
as been secluding myself in my home as of

recent and why the reason i suppose needed
to watch her radiant and graceful figure every
single solitary move and motion only those
cute and adorable girls are capable of running
away full of gusto into town fading stick figure
disappearing to the horizon with no return
route and was able to completely relate
and be sympathetic and run away
with her in mind body and spirit

9.

tonight my wife had finally had it and kicked in my door
and threw a butterfly net over my head. i didn't put up
much of a fight as was sympathetic and fluttered
a bit and stuck a pin right in my chest and hung
me up with the rest of the pests. my arms and
legs have been flapping for some time now and
must admit am getting a bit tired and think have
finally learned my lesson and could use a seltzer
and have really gotten to appreciate and gain full
perspective to realize how unimportant is sports
and weather and how good it feels to be irrelevant
and can hear her giggling a little in the background
how she thinks it's funny that every time *fast times
at ridgemont high* comes on i watch it but who
would turn down fast times at ridgemont high
like macaroons or beer nuts and do finally
at last get where she's at and will stay
up here as long as she sees fit

10.

on this clear-cut dawn
the boy on the moon
leans his ladder up
against the stars

what else can
he really do
but keep on? special
on cold cuts and
chicken thighs
at the polish
market on
the river
in brooklyn
where they
keep the fog
horns and
merchant
marine
veterans
and you
thankfully
got no one
and no one
to turn to and
stick your head
out the window
to your best friends
dead dolls in the alley
the best way to read
the weather
and tides

your moods
your blues
your lull
a-byes.

Charlie

My crazy paratrooping painting boss
used to do crazy shit like when I was
on top of the ladder would say–"What's
taking you so long?" and literally pick
me up and start moving me along
and when time and life was killing
us and just getting way too bored
would just pull down his pants
with his balls hanging out
and swing his paintbrush
and then after the job was
done finish off cases of beer
in the basement swerving home
always making observations
and statements about strangers
on the road saying shit like
you can tell that girl's got
problems and at the end
of the week always got
paid under the table
a great big wad of money
just enough to get myself
into trouble during the summer
to pick up a couple bags of ganja
from my connection called Bronx
runs and meet them outside their
tenements on the corner who at
the time felt like the only reliable people.
Charlie always talked about one day retiring
and making it down to his paradise in the sun
to some condo in Florida where he wouldn't
be bothered and go fishing from morning
to sundown and sure as hell hope he made
it down there raising hell and creating his
own private mayhem as one of those
minor characters and few old timers
who in my opinion surely did deserve it.

When I got home and showered
still a bit dizzy with a buzz on
I just naturally thought about
that girl with the problems.

Plant City, FLA

The ball flies off the bat
and jesus christ in center
field goes dashing after it
trying desperately to track
it in the sun and just lands
over his outstretched arms
like some old jew or sicilian
from the old country or farmer
praying to god pleading for rain
while nothing else he can do but
watch it bounce from the warning
track right over the center field fence
into soft blissful anonymous oblivion
right below those gorgeous swaying
sheltering palms like exotic fezzes
blowing in the breeze where retirees
very pleasantly mutely head towards
their air-conditioned paradise down
the pale pristine highway to the gates
of eden; turns out as always a perfect
day in the mid-70's in clearwater, fla.
with some billboard which shows a
large frankfurter reading something
like "quite frankly" all the young
pretty lactating lily-white girls
smiling from the crowd with
their newborn daughters
and if that hardworking
workhorse of a reliever
with the sleazy handle
bar mustache doesn't
make it will go back
to his off-season
position working
in the adult movie industy
jesus actually quite sympathetic
cause knows somehow just needs
to make a living and support a family
and really not hurting anybody; a little

later on, ironically, prophetically christ
knocks on the door of one of the broad
casters and asks if he might somewhere
in the near to remote future have him
read his elegy, as always loved his stimulating
voice, sense of humor, and even bedside manner
just to possibly hold off on all those long-winded
stories and parables, as well as anecdotes of him
trying to make it and his struggles in the minors
for in retrospect the most romantic and nostalgic.

Like Screaming Plankton

i wood have
want dead
to have scene
that batman
& robin epi-
sode where
he blows
his brains out
all over the wall
& next scene
simply shows
him with a
sardonic
smile
clutching
the suicide
note cameras
showing a close-
up of the joker
with sincere
tears in his
eyes and
taking off
in silence
to stage
right
wood have
want dead
to have
scene
that epi-
sode where
they show
g.i. joe who
as a kid you
eternally thought
would save the world
& in your imagination
did in his camouflage

chiseled with five o'clock
shadow & that
very compact
pose kneeling
on one knee
with that bazooka
joe who always
suspiciously had
that turtleneck
pulled up over
his pie hole like
some grandiose
petty thief with
a trick up his
sleeve & great
wise ass dreams
wood have want
dead to have
scene
that epi-
sode
where
they just
show the
ghosts
& mists
& fogs
& stray
animals
sleep-
walking
past
your
window
wood have
want dead
to have
scene
that
epi-
sode

where you
& your
best friend
followed
that babbling
brook in winter
through backyards
of the suburbs spying
& peeking in on madmen
neighbors to the holy
source of the
bronx river
wood have
want dead
to have
scene
that
epi-
sode
where
ralph & lenny
your gardeners
growing up like
real-life *mice & men*
characters father & son
dynamic duo from the old
& new country of sicilia
the former, old, stocky,
stubbly in his immigrant
fisherman's hat
& the latter
strong & sculpted
what hard work
will do to you with-
out an ounce of fat
self-effacing & silent
your mentors
growing up
because
they always
showed up

i wood have
want dead
to have
scene
that epi-
sode of
that parrot
who parrots
his owner
an out-
of-work
lounge
singer
& develops
a heroin
habit
& be-
comes
a dope
attic
nodding
out in his
cage all
day long
wood have
want dead
to have
scene
that epi-
sode where
they mouth
fuck every
reality
show
cunt-
test-
aint
& they
finally just
choke on it
& shut the fuck

up wood have
want dead
to have
scene
that epi-
sode where
the old man
finally decides
to throw his hat
in the ring
& instead
flings his
whole body
creaky bones
& all off the
brooklyn bridge
followed by
holy bliss-
ful black kids
doing back-
flips off
the board-
walk
inn
coney
island
wood have
want dead
to have
scene
that epi-
sode where
during the
deaf dumb
& blind
debates
one of the
candy-
dates
just
simply

loses it
& ass-
sin hates
them all
& the cus-
toad ian
shows
up with
his crime
& punish
meant
push-
broom
&
un-
be-
livable
wage
& does
some-
thing
worth-
while
in these
higher-
than-
holy
half-
crazed
united
states
full
of
shit
poor
taste
&
chor-
oreo-
graphed
rage

to know
this is neither
world-federated
wrestling
weather
with more
catastrophic
climate change
winds & tornadoes
blowing from some-
where between texas
& the midwest where
they keep all those
evangelicals
conveniently
stocked for the
upcoming elections
nor a test of your patience
& emergency broadcast system.

    Mock Apple Pie

1

The patterns of history & civilization
prove very much to be triggers
from social and cultural and
psychological and spiritual
man's petty absurd cruelty
to man where the symbolic
becomes quite literal
and literal symbolic

2

One wonders if government and politics
is as bad as it was in greek and roman times
as in my opinion a comparison may be made just
in much different ways (but when you think about
it really not so much) while all forms of subjugation
and lies and betrayal and deals and abuses of power

why the rise of the great philosopher (& rebel & scholar)
all having to go into hiding or put on trial by the devils
pleading for their beliefs & ideas & rights & lives

3

Words speak louder than actions...

4

If you asked me how the world began
i would tell you it's when all the gods
randomly all of a sudden spontaneously
fainted and bit the dust and it all sprang
up from their powerful and sorrowful

solemn brooding bodies as archetypes
came to life and when they gradually
fluttered off and crossed the border
to the netherworld somewhere
between the conscious and
unconscious world this is when
the world developed all its natural
geological traits and characteristics
and formations and came into being

that sole solitary survivor explorer being
standing proud stranded deserted abandoned
on the edge of the precipice looking out to the horizon

winds coming in and soon
will be the blessed rain
all in the shape of...

5

Imagine churchill wiping his mug off
after one of those yalta conferences
with one of those wet warm towels
they used to give you at the end
of those feasts at one of those
good ole chinese restaurants

(why do theodore roosevelt
and howard taft with that great
big taffy smile never get talked about?)

6

I think kafka lived in one of those
pure plastic pods and saw it all
from the poor helpless portholes
of one of those beatdown bubblegum
machines surrounded by other plastic
things then some punk random stranger

slipped a quarter in and he'd go tumbling
against his own will and volition
forced to have to figure it all out

this is how he developed
wisdom and a sixth sense

jean-paul sartre's
'nausea' was contagious...

7

I should have gotten a letter of recommendation
for college from my detention hall monitor

"don't give my sen-sen to the schizophrenics!
it was a gift from my sister!"

vote trump for the ticket
vote hillary for the ticket

fuck it! anyone ever attempted
to take them hostage before it?

take out their campaign manager?
those automatons from their smiling choir?

reminds me of one of those relatives i'd never
think of talking to at a family get-together or function

8

Recently
not really
have had
a fantasy
of one
of those
beautiful

and sleazy
aristocratic
southern belles
in her hoop dress
with a slight glimpse
of her pale buttocks
and seductive whip
even have her parasol
up with deep thick humidity
and magnolia seeping through
the shutters trust me have
been there and done that
with some of the cutest
insane jewish girls
from the suburbs

9

History of this country's a crime
and don't fool yourself still runs
by a herd-like mob mentality
an obvious and see-through
and predictable trend where
people desperately try to fit
in and cater (and acclimate)
to that privileged and entitled
mediocre majority baseline

10

There was a reason
for organized crime
coming from a very unfair
and unjust disorganized life

like some fucked-up
dysfunctional game
of musical chairs

doing the hokey-pokey
turning yourself around

11

Always seemed to make a name for myself
every time someone tried to steal
my name from myself

12

Is it just me (know it's not)
but does it not just seem like
the whole world's melting away
and breaking apart while arrogant
and aloof suits at ball games are
busy on their smart phones texting
away and america online providing
all these tips and suggestions to
pour coca-cola in your fertilizer
to help your garden grow?

13

Always find myself picking up hitch hikers along the road
and pretty nice and down to earth people and will take
them for miles on end and as far as they want to go
or can take them as totally sympathetic as not just
about their car breaking down but their life breaking
down and family breaking down and i was exactly
just like them and it's scenes like these where have
always felt closest to culture in these interludes
and moments and even now any chance i can
will head and crossover the border to check
them out check out that second language
you were mandated to take a long time ago
and now find myself rather fluent in remedial

14

Why does it always seem like those
who need and require peace and solitude
the most have the hardest time in finding it
and eventually may even be put in the pathetic
unenviable absurd category of 'undesirable' or 'violent'

15

Cul-de-sacs, dead ends, homeowner's associations, and suburbia
are like really bad predictable strolls through overly-manicured
neighbor/hoods of nepotism as ironically have always
felt far safer in very dangerous unfamiliar areas

16

Pain,
shame,
sane,
saint

i've lost my strength
lost my memory
what did ya say?

17

Are the people
in the haunted
house also
haunted?

18

The sign along the side of the road
reads "pain ahead" snicker to myself
going–"tell me something i don't know"

jim morrison in
the background–
"unhappy girl..."

19

You drift through tourist towns
while through hard knocks
and experience have
learned to naturally
ignore them as
they're all simply
repeated cookie-cutter
cowards who just greedily
take and got nothing to offer

they feel like the expression
'the white slave trade'

20

GI joe trooper
literally standing
in sun glasses
and uniform
and ten-gallon
secretly hiding
in the shadows
of the shrubs
of some
front lawn
in this very

quaint historic town
pointing his radar gun
right at your car when
you're just picking up
speed to accelerate
to try and get out

what the hell is this all about
and who are the real criminals?

chuck d said–"america
is set up to trap you…"

21

Freedom (is what it feels like)
to finally be left the hell alone
when they don't know you
and finally get home…

Kinney Drugs: the life cycle

At the drug store in the strip mall
it's like a cross between folklore and war
morbidly-obese lady puts up her handicap
parking ticket as if to accommodate for her
extra-large buttocks, like carrying around twins
and then indifferently zaps her car alarm as if beaming
up in this oh so dangerous parking lot, while the farmer
with his built-in, soiled dungarees looks around, disoriented
and confused then instantly forgets like he has been forced
to and goes through his daily routines and rituals, and gets
into his pickup and takes off past the pre-cut kindling and
firewood and vanishes into thin air; the very kind good-
hearted stick figure high school girls, a bit paranoid and
guarded depart with their very safe and secure perfectly
prudent and prudish organized steps as if planning
for their near future along the straight and narrow
carrying tiny plastic bags of feminine sundries
then self-consciously, modestly, take-off
like alabaster angels; males with their
idiot and obvious bully demonstrations
in the demographic between the ages
of 15 and late 20's exhibit the compulsive
need and competitive pattern to always have
to land a lugie to stake out their alpha-male
territory; old timers, male and female gender-
oriented, carry out their gallon of milk and
supply of toilet paper, respectively, while those
drug store castle doors magically open and close
by their own volition when they sense and detect
there's a human being near the premises (to
welcome all of civilization) into the vestibule
all decked-out with bottles and bottles of blue
windshield wiper fluid and rock salt to assault
and attract the masses, everything they could
possibly want and need to make it through
the season and existence and this
reality of functioning and being.

Friendly's

There are some things i miss
about the lower east side
like that really nice barber
i used to see on delancey
her name was linette
and was puerto rican
and used to call her
linette the barberette
and she was young
and good looking
with a good sense
of humor and had
a brother in prison
in a picture frame
with his tattoos
and muscles
and great big
proud smile
almost looking
like a graduation photo
camped-out on the counter
where she kept all her scissors
and combs and clippers in that jar
of blue liquid and said got time for
robbing a whole chain of *friendly's*
in the upstate area. when i inquired
a little further and asked if he had
held up anywhere else she very naturally
with a slight and subtle smile responded
"no just the friendly's, that wasn't very
friendly was it?" but it was intriguing
cuz she and her brother strangely
enough both seemed far more
happy than me while i shuffled
out all by lonesome something
i savored those days with a nice
shave under the manhattan bridge
to the river to get my head straight.

Wanda

In checking on my bank balance
during the hi-holy days listening
to this god awful muzac where
couldn't even pin down the original
song waiting for a specialist from
an award-winning bank or award
winning specialist or whatever
other crap america addresses
it as wanda finally got on the phone
and asked me what she could help
me with as was positive i was over
my limit and a little embarrassed
and wanda in her very optimistic
tone of voice she was trained with
announced—"i have some very good
news for you..." as was expecting
out of the clear blue sky one of those
breakthroughs or bizarre bureaucratic
miracles where i had forgotten i had
two hundred more bucks left to play
around with wanda declared 'you are
not overdrawn and have a dollar and
eighteen cents' yet somehow this did
not feel like particularly good news
while somehow from all the theater
of the absurd and patterns of damage
and abuse would have more so preferred
to hear some crazy shit something like
you are overdrawn by so and so and
you're on your own as i don't know
just didn't feel particularly uplifting
or inspiring to me that i have a dollar
and eighteen cents left to my name
as she asked me if i needed help
with anything else this award-
winning specialist from this
award-winning bank and said
something to the effect of no thanks
you've been very helpful and think may
have even called her by her first name.

The Complaint Department

I called back one of these idiot internet companies and went to
that part of the screen where it speaks of "technical difficulties"
may have even been one of those fucked-up commercials where
people are always constantly dancing around hysterically and out
of control thinking shit's gonna save them and improve their
lifestyle and gonna get this object or trend sent to their home
and one of those cookie-cutter clones with their choreographed
script and prepackaged dialogue gets on the phone and says–
"thank you for calling, how may we help you today?" like they're
all a part of some great big family and if you follow the exact rules
you too can be part of the group, as i suddenly responded only
the way someone is capable of who's just been around the block
way too much and sick of it all and don't want to hear bullshit
anymore, and tell this kid–"the coo-coo clock you assholes
sent me won't stop coughing" and acting shocked and startled
and finally getting this automaton out of his coma at last some-
thing he's not trained to do goes–"excuse me sir, what did you
say?" and resenting how they always turn so patronizing and
formal i said "the coo-coo clock you faggots sent me won't stop
coughing" then they always seem to get personally offended and
defensive like–"sir i can help you but don't appreciate the rude
language" as if i was even aiming it at him and meaning it on that
level as never ever been like that and have best friends and family
members of that gender, but more casual and colloquial and have to
calm their temper-tantrum, and after a little self-soothing and
reframing goes instantly back to being this mechanical zombie and
doing what he spiritually believes to be his job, started asking me
for my personal information which of course always includes like
an address or phone number and microscopic model number, and
like some schmuck or slave to the system proceeded to repeat my
complaint verbatim–"customer reports coo-coo clock won't stop
coughing" and gave me all my options (which of course only gets
me angrier and more frustrated) and what i will have to do to get
this defective coo-coo back to them and always resentful that i got
to do all the leg work and they're consistently a bunch of fuck-ups
and my transitional-object just not doing its job of which all i
hoped for would coo-coo on the hour to help me get to bed and
somehow count down my time on earth and mortality while i
routinely sink into my series of nightmares and found myself

wrapping up this coo-coo clock strapping masking tape all around his mouth, as if gagging him and taking him hostage although knew he had absolutely nothing to do with it and started to reflect how i hope i don't miss hearing him gasping and coughing at 1, 2, 3 in the morning...

The Ancient Lagoon Business Park Of The Future

Where i live up on top
of the dead wood of
ancient trees in
the prehistoric
lagoon where
the pick-up
stick legs
of egrets
hang out to
contemplate
the seasons
with the fresh
scents of burning
magnolia and cedar
somewhere between
the stars and nocturnal
creatures i tinker away
all day contented
with the keen stray
aroma of gunpowder
and formaldehyde and
lemon meringue pie
where i believe out
here in america
through the pine
they are putting in
a new business park
with white suburban
housewives instantly
clicking on their
car alarms as a
part of their body
language and every
day routine and ritual
and what it means
to belong strolling
into the climate
controlled tinted
windows of heaven

married to cut-throat
climbers and serial killers
right around where they
just put in those f-35
bombers doing mock
kamikaze nosedives
right over the very
neat and tidy rows
of cookie-cutter
condominiums
scaring the hell
out of its citizens
as you look down
focused, centered
from atop the dead
wood in the lagoon
waiting for your
loved one
getting local
anesthesia.
you started
the morning
off with telling
a cop playing
god to go fuck
himself which
felt so cathartic
while in america
felt like freedom
and knew he wasn't
gonna do anything
about it cuz didn't
have the street
smarts and
caught him
off guard and
little shocked
playing god
reason why
i've become
an agnostic

as your wife
starts to doze
off in the last
of the summer
sun somer
saulting
back through
the neat trailer
parks and farms
to a place which
might resemble
something like
shangrila...

On Darwin, Or Plankton And The Origins Of The Ecosystem

1

the true difference between the male and female
of the species is that the female is able to nurse
her young while the male nurses his beer trying
to make the high last as long as he possibly can

2

one can speak in-depth as well on the self
same subject of the nature of the orgasm

3

on 'tension-fatigue syndrome' and how stress
and anxiety eventually gets you in the long-run

4

on how the anatomical system breaks down
for no apparent reason and leaves one feeling
cursed, spiritually/physiologically to depression

5

after breakups one experiences the strange sensation
of feeling both filthy and empty and at that exact moment
are confused wondering if in retrospect it was lust or love
(or just something behavioral you got used to) triggering
you way back to something which happened a very long
time ago, causing you to put down your glove in the school-
yard; a certain type of lost innocence which during that stage
of growth and development or circumstance of living really
had absolutely nothing (and everything) to do with you

6

you never really know how lonely loneliness is
until you have a similar period to look back at it

7

once you start believing the doubters you're dead forever

8

in between dying do that strange thing called living

9

develop habits or rituals or what they
like to refer to as customs and hobbies

(you always got confused by such probing
and really felt mind your own freakin' business)

10

how paranoia is not always just psychotic
but a reality-based defense-mechanism
based on patterns and experience

11

the core nucleus of truth is surrounded by hypocrisy
and contradiction constantly trying to break in...

12

it is imperative to take a vacation when you least expect it...
when you start to pick up these symptoms and has absolutely
nothing to do with being impulsive but mature and introspective

13

traveling includes as much the sensation and phenomenon
of being on-the-run existentially having lost the concept of home

14

we can obviously speak about our failing schools and education
in america but this goes all the way to the universities where one
has to 'practically' be a conformist to fit in and become a part of
the system and fraternities and sororities and if not and a true free
thinker (does that or can that even exist anymore?) or independent
thinker instantly made to feel distant and ashamed and alienated
which may lead to a sort of situational depression and 'ridiculous'
melancholia (when their hearts and souls were originally in it)

15

most doctors are not trained in the most basic and fundamental
and elemental of ways which is simple bedside manner (and 95%
of the game) and may be precocious or geniuses (often clinically
narcissistic even sociopathic) but clueless when it comes to the
human condition and being empathic and compassionate and
more times than not can even exacerbate the problem or through
a clinical abuse of power, believe it or not, come up with a whole
new one of its own...

16

google should have aerial cameras which come down
and zoom in on the manic damaged and suffering soul

17

i'm not so sure anymore how much i believe in god
while at the end of the day a guy needs to drop to
his knees and pray and start crying by his wife's
bedside so he might really show her how sorry...
how much he appreciates and needs and loves her

18

of course obviously there was brando in 'streetcar'
what was that movie with jimmy cagney where
he was in prison? you look up to the ceiling
and start considering praying to god...

19

lying in bed in the deep dark night you hear the downpour
and with that as well always the sweet rapturous
symphony of the cicadas and tree frogs

20

when the stones came out with their first couple of albums
half of them were covers to black blues singers from america–
'baby back, dressed in black, silver buttons up and down her back...
then i said hi like a spider to a fly...' and in my opinion had just
as much mad heart (and gusto) as their classics yet mick jagger
somehow developing this weird thick deep southern
accent having gone to the london school of economics

21

one does not really know silence until after a hell of a lot of
suffering and unnecessary judgment and then can feel and
hear and see and smell every detail of the senses and seasons

22

the man in the comic book shop stole my wife
and just left breadcrumbs to remember her by

23

i want my ashes scattered anywhere else besides some lake or ocean
or mountain but maybe that mcdonald's me and my friends used
to hang out in in the mall, that diner my buddy and i used to go
to by the train station of *metro north* when all the trains came
rattling in from grand central and got a real true-blue feeling
of the seasons, that *7-11* parking lot and in the window the
back of boxes of prophylactics, cigarettes, and baseball
cards, when that window was slightly open in french
class and all you smelt was the mud and marigolds
where i first heard she had a crush on me in the
locker room of my high school, autumn in cloisters by
the heather gardens with a breathtaking explorer's view
of the hudson where i first courted her, those woods of
winter where my first love and i used to take midnight
strolls along the silhouetted river and powdered twinkling
trees by the cathedral, the south of france when i finally
got away from the madness of it all and the healing holy
palms of the mediterannean which just suddenly showed
up out of nowhere like a miracle through my window of
the *tgv* from paris to nice, slow trains from the big easy, sevilla
and the whitewashed cliffs of santorini during the off-season.

Wendy's

When i used to work out there
i used to live at a welfare hotel
with a bunch of drag queens
and alkies and losers
and cold-blooded killers
and literal fugitives on-the-run
from the reservations of montana
to the lush shores of oregon
where i had absolutely
no one to rely on
and used to take a bus all the way
out there through the maddening
weather to the wealthy suburbs
to be harassed and hassled
by this little hoity-toity girl
in high school some perfect
miserable good deed doer
with all this attitude who
i guess had reached the high ranks
of assistant manager and was like
some nazi expecting you to obey
and devote your life and follow
the exact rules and regulations
and one time during clean-up
during one of those really
dreary dusks a buddy
of mine who i think
was just kind of being
kind and sympathetic
took the leftover fries
from the fryer which
were being dumped
and then filled up
some bag for me
(which i thought was
a real nice gesture for
my trip home) and think
to teach me some sort of
lesson or another she swiped

the bag right out my hand and
tossed them right into the garbage can
as though teaching some sort of ridiculous
lesson and believe may have even given me
a lecture as was directly against some store
policy and was starving and i was like
you gotta be kidding? like this girl
was in high school and this is how
they train them these days?

Is this what they refer
to as the american way?

So apparently out here
in america they care more
about policy than hierarchy of needs?

Turned out they made those infamous
junior cheeseburgers simply by taking
it and cutting it in half with a spatula.

On The State Of The Game

You sit back in your
easy chair in your
dark room under
a full moon high
up in the stars nursing
a cold one meant for your
wife's best friend husband
of course they never show
up and enjoy it that much
more while suddenly
a commercial comes
on over your television
which tells you about
all those opportunities
in the state of new york
and think looks good
and pretty damn cool
and all of a sudden
forget that's where
you're from and start
to feel a little down
in the dumps and
find it a kind of a mild
tragedy how basketball
is no longer a team sport
(but seems more like a dunk-
a-thon where they try to embarrass
and show off and gloat and then all
repetitive and monochromatic-like
whether black or white lift their
caveman skulls to the rafters
to howl out loud like some king
of the jungle) and feel a little
let down as not the way
you were brought up
to play the sport
(ibid: the blood-thirsty
coaches looking like
sadistic ringmasters;

that chorus line of
cheerleaders seated
on the court with their
pom-poms moving in
hypnotic, cyclical, ritualistic
motion, like neon going off
at a vegas casino; the mascot
texting, the seedy and vulgar
country club alumni all lined-
up in a neat little row in their
sweater vests of course the color
of their team colors, and the whole
audience looking like the crowd
at the coliseum digging the slaughter
going in for the kill; another commercial
comes on showing one of those mini applicators
which will instantly make him look years younger
as he immediately like a miracle turns eternally
happy and cocky and confidant, and think you
always liked them so much more before than
after and do they have one where they can
just put the gray back in?) and sip a little
more at your homegrown beer feeling a
bit colder like hanging out at one of those
keg parties way back in the day in high
school in some chilly autumnal backyard
not really liking the taste at all but getting
much quicker and clever and impressing
all the girls playing the role of the clown
and comedian yet strangely enough feeling
more removed and a stranger and always
returning home alone stoned skulking
the shadows buzzed and wasted
somewhere in that strange state
of mind between fantasy and reality
knowing exactly who you were but not
really and find it by no coincidence how
everything truly does come around full circle.

A Different Sort Of Manifesto (manifest destiny)

1,

all i can kind of tell you
   is that life & existence
      kind of seems like
         all that small print
            i don't care to read

2,

all those tiny
     microscopic & magical
        creatures from evolution
           i see in passing
              after being pulled
                  under the undertow

3,

having revelations
     after being tossed drunk
        slow-motion
           through the window
              of *white castle*

4,

i never saw my whole life
     pass right in front of me
        but like always
           saw right through them
              & their false sympathy

5,

scenes from the pharmacy
        & a food fight

    which suddenly
           breaks out
                at the chinese buffet
                      for no explicit reason
                            spending the rest
                      of the evening
              reading dostoevsky
casually contemplating
        all those cornfields
                of dusk
which got you home
            in one piece
                  as if any of that shit
                mattered
        or was even relevant

6,

everything must go sale
                around the gaslight
                          cobblestone mission

   the phlebotomist & methadone clinic
                the foghorns & steeples

where ironically
        all's fragile & forgotten

        somewhere between
the embezzlers & jesus

              the heathen politicians

7,

                stray dogs
once man's best friend

                apparently not
     good enough friends
& not really men

8,

accents created
through just straight-
up suffering & survival
mechanisms & states of
mind find ourselves in

9,

                  that brother howling
                           at his sister
                                    beneath the rainy
        marquee of the movie theater–
                  "i'm not proud i'm a dope addict!"

              planning secret heists
          & escape routes
     & itineraries

to the pearly gates
          of hell
                   with no way home

10,

like the bittersweet ending
of streetcar, long day's journey
into night & death of a salesman

(can assure you kafka, shakespeare
& louis-ferdinand celine was in no
way shape or form a coincidence)

11,

        like all that preparation
            (put in)
                of drag queens

     no different
        & the exact same ritual
               & routine

    of wealthy women
       from the suburbs

      all simply
  about the presentation

(trying on faces
    doing impersonations & impressions)

12,

no different than the ushers
        or patrons
            than the phantoms

13,

(as an addendum & an aside
could never stand the state
of mind of the eccentric
who always came across
or felt like some built-in
excuse for arrogance,
self-absorption & really
poor character & behavior
thriving off rationalizations

14,

strange & fucked-up thing about human nature
they never ever seem to really appreciate your
confessions always coming from the most
sincere & honest & modest of places
& with this repetition of behavioral
patterns perversely appear to turn
resentful as if you were just making
excuses & were literally baring it all
for assholes who never really deserved
it in the first place & never see them
again & in retrospect thank the lord)

15,

in america, love to poke fun at one-hit wonders
but at least they had their day in the sun, girls in
tight, painted-on, slut-polyester dance pants, wagging
their fingers at boys during bar-mitzvahs during that song
by donna summer & barbra streisand "enough is enough"
& we're like what the fuck? what could we have done
at such a young age to exact such venom? our 13
year old entrance into manhood & what we had
to look forward to in the near & remote future

16,

hold tight
   onto the toboggan
      & girl by your side

  don't tug too hard
    & just gently glide

    be her guide
      but more importantly
        let her guide you

        through rough
& ridiculous times

17,

if i ever make my millions
first thing i'm gonna buy
are one of those gazebos,
a lifetime subscription
to national geographic
& saturday evening post,
field & stream & playboy

18,

  as a boy trying to read
            all those directions
                        in spanish
                                  just for the fuck of it

& still coming up
        with the perfect jumbo jetliner
                balanced up on top
                        my childhood dresser
                              high on model glue

        you know the ones
                which always went down
                        never quite made it

                            & people kept on taking
            in that strange decade
        of the seventies

19,

all's you really need
in the long-run is a

window far enough
away from it all
to observe
the passing
the changing
of the brutal &
delicate seasons

20,

the graceful beauty
           of her body
ponytail bobbing
        along with the cadence
                      & rhythm
of her long-distance
             running

that lit flashing beacon
         at the head of the bicycle
                     gradually drifting
& penetrating through the evening

21,

the path the fog takes
        in the morning
              slipping
                   down
                         the mountain

22,

separating truth from all
those false truths they try to so
blatantly bullshit & brainwash
you as being reality & virtue

(in some ways a form of abuse
which can instantly be disproved)

23,

                i was the one always found
           lost in translation
      caught between tenses

     giving great long elegies
 of pillow talk

        whispering sweet nothings
           into the ear of my one-
                night stand mistress

           cracking one-liners at funerals
                predicting the future

24,

can't believe those centerfielders
              i grew up with
                    & loved & idolized...

          cleon jones from the mets
       & kirby puckett from the twins
   eventually got nailed for some sort
of sexual perpetration

25,
         to know when those old
 idiot alpha-male managers
                  come storming out
                      the dugout
                  to go head to head
             toe to toe
        with the umpire
that is the perfect metaphor
        & about as far

                        as we'll ever go
      with civilization
            with male-bonding

26,

      "it's a saturday night and i ain't got nobody..."

You Got Me Babe

i liked when you used to make
those awkward phone calls
as a boy for some reason
all anxious and nervous
finding yourself humming
something like before
she got on as if placating
a romantic heart–"all along
the waterfall with you...
my brown-eyed girl..."
looking back and reflecting
it felt so freudian and then
when she got on really
didn't have too much
to talk about and
couldn't say what
you really wanted
to say; sometimes
they'd catch you
mouthing those
words and say–
"what'ya say?"

"no, nothing..."

Maturity

you get so lonesome
you start looking up
girls you used to
dry-fuck at keg
parties; interestingly
they look just as
desperate and
sleazy and
all ended
up marrying
some sort of
bond salesmen
or another.
you wonder
where it all
went wrong
but know it's
got absolutely
nothing to do
with any that

You imagine the image
of one of those *hollywood squares*
nodding-out and them simply passing him up.

Stanzas Of Youth

1

I remember when
i was real young
and in high
school and got
into studio 54
and this older
girl came up
from behind
me and squeezed
my butt and spent
the rest of the night
trying to find her
and how that
flattery and
futile mission
seemed like
the grand
metaphor
for it all

2

Tony Manero
played by
john travolta
in *saturday
night fever*
when he
was ordering
a cheeseburger
and french fries
and a cup of
coffee at that
diner with
that greaser

girl from
bayside
and she
tries to
impress
him
and
talks
about
the film
romeo & juliet
and he responds
yeah that was
written by
shakespeare
and she says
no zefferelli!
and instantly
real quick
and street
wise
snaps
you know
i think that
romeo drank
the poison
way too fast
which was
hilarious
and think
says it
all about
woman
and man

3

Biggie from
bed stuy.
brooklyn

& p. diddy
declared
'i don't
want no
crying
at my
funeral.'

A Bio Starting Somewhere From The Middle

I remember living in the dangerous French Quarter of New
Orleans and all of a sudden one night in one of those empty
and abandoned streets seeing some bum literally heave another
bum straight through the window based on a quarrel over a
puppy and believe in retrospect and upon reflection like twenty
years later felt something like the opposite of birth with glass
shattered all over the curb and after helping him up all bloody
and cut-up nothing could have felt more vacant and I guess
that exact phase or period where you lose all your innocence
completely unaware of it.

Where I'm from in New York people just naturally
walk with their heads over their shoulders and remember
one day this traveling carnival coming up from behind me
I swear on Delancey and finally able to move forward
realizing at that moment it all just being the theater
of the absurd or as Bob Marley so prophetically put it–
"Lord I got to keep on moo-ving where I can't be found."

About a decade later you find yourself brooding
out the 12th floor window of the empty cafeteria
at Yeshiva to become a social worker looking
out at all of upper-Manhattan and mad streets
and when I mean mad I really mean mad real
life hustle of Washington Heights and the beauty
and craziness of Cloisters my first year of internship
having an affair with a borderline woman in the middle
of a divorce and learned more than you will ever begin
to know about the female gender and my second year
meeting the girl I really loved still living with her mother
in The Bronx until you realize it's all just needy and
necessary distractions from all the fucked-up bullshit
and bureaucracy of humanity and find deep-down
inside pretty damn shallow people are maddening
as simply just going to do what they're going to do.

You wonder if in looking back you really miss
all this or as the brothers put it–"Just trying
to make it" and only sick of all the repetition.

Schmuck

I walked into the Freudian
and the first thing he said to me
was 'first thing that comes to mind'

I opined "schmuck!"
and felt like a new man.

Mental Health

It's a weird business...like you can't even walk down the hall without offending someone. and they're your fellow therapists. (like he was undressing me with his non-verbals. i'm a vegan. i'm experiencing counter-transference from a domineering father-figure. the type who always use the word "comfortable" and don't feel comfortable with them constantly using the word comfortable. the ones who would always rat on you in school) and then you get spoken to for like a half-hour by some bullshit supervisor full of psychobabble who you don't trust and the biggest hypocrite and asshole of them all who'd take you into his confidence and ask who on the treatment team you think swallows. you honestly couldn't care less and are just indifferent and not that interested, nor for that matter, hostile. he tells you we have a special relationship and you think really? this is what you call a special relationship? and feel more so violated like one of those people who constantly flatters you you have no respect for.at the treatment plan meeting he passes around pictures of his wife and kids from their vacation they just took to the caribbean.

Stand-Ins

the one
thing
you
learn
about
the
ho
tell
business
is that
real
shallow
classless
idiots
can
climb
the
lad
her
of
suck
cess
cunt
sider
guests
mobs
snobs
slobs
flocks of
drunken
middle
aged
women
who
never
shut
the
fuck up
trying

to seduce
& torture
the front
desk
clerk
&
bell
men
on long
week
ends
too
passive
aggressively
get back
at their
husbands
for the
very safe
& secure
existence
they always
wanted &
now resentful
for/given
every
thing
they
ever
wanted
husbands
good family
men coming
in from the
midwest
picking
up drag
queens
from
meat
market

where
rabbis
also
hang out
trying to
sneak
them
up to
their
beds
quiet
as a rat
i mean
mouse
farm
pseudo
call &
cosmo
tologist
conventions
where you
just gotta
get an 80%
on the test
loud &
obnoxious
intoxicated
college girls
very pure
un adult
rated
daddy's
little
girls
bunch
of whore
conformists
doing it all
doing all
the same
positions

for the sake
of the sorority
so they can
one day
be just as
accepted
& alienating
brainwashed
jocks having
become
schlock
salesmen
all repeating
the same bullshit
what's been spoon
fed to them
from what
the country
club cult quota
quoted them
disoriented
lawyers
pathetically
trying to
make it
on the
elevator
like
taking
their
first
steps
up
the
lad
her
of
suck
cess.

Hospitality

Anacronyms fighting anacronyms for clarification
until you leave the interrogation room confused
quixotic and cryptic being written up for not
following the exact telemarketer script as
using your natural instincts over the phone
making the client feel comfortable and welcome
(having been listened in on by big brother/grand
inquisitor who I guess in this situation/incident
sides with management for using your natural
instinct/natural charm major cause for alarm)
having sacrificed everything for them now
deemed as 'suspicious' and something of
a 'criminal' being escorted out by security
(for litigious reasons, supposedly a part of
the same union) through different subterranean
tunnels and a different exit you never even
knew existed and guess in this instance
don't work anymore so much as a team
or family member (sort of ironic and
a perverse psychological phenomenon
because first time you felt it) and the last
thing you remember was waving goodbye
to the timekeeper you had never met before
pretty nice fellow and then show you the door.

```
Have A Cigar
```

I've gotten to the point in interviews where I don't even
try, and imagine *myself* naked, spewing small talk & lies

watching that opaque sun slanting through
the windows of the cafe at the train station.

This one's for the hospitality business and ironically
used to work next door at the schizophrenic residence

where they'd smoke butts in the back and howl
right on time like clockwork drowned out

by the clitter-clatter of trains when they'd
come barreling in in the early evening. .

The managers used to do nothing trained to ignore them
wanting to get in their runs as had relationship problems

the nasty nurses showing up at their own convenience
who had ins with them I guess 'cause they had licenses

and looking to write you up for the smallest shit
while literally just worked a double-shift for them.

The Graveyard

I think i want to get
one of those jobs
where you like
deliver people's
internal organs
back & forth
between hospitals
as might just give
my life a little
purpose
& meaning
but knowing
my luck
& history
will probably
end up towing
my sorry ass
back & forth
with people's
melting hearts
& souls
& kidneys
& spleens.

Overcast (with a chance)

Those motel
bathrooms
where you
decide how
much you
love her
where you
decide how
much you
really love
yourself?

Somewhere between
life & death; best place
to catch the weather
to have reservations

Somewhere between
reflection & escapism
a certain sense of relief
from situational depression.

Sans Title

how to play
dominoes
on the
sleeping
spine of
the thin
girl with
flaming
hair you
always
pined
& adored
in that little
motel off
the coast
of glou-
cester.

For W. Burroughs

i could never ever stand those self-made men
as they always act and got that look on their
face like i'm a self-made man or look more
like allegories or parables or examples
this is what it is to be a self-made man
and more so look to me like a bunch
of fucken scams (and all i'm thinking
i want to slug them right in the freaken
nose and level them these self-made men)
while everyone's always talking about
how they got so much respect fawning
over their reputations (and can almost
guarantee you some of the filthiest shit
they did to gain it and can see straight
through to their hypocrisies and con-
tradictions) and get to thinking what
the hell does that even mean anyway?
a self-made man? like you made yourself
up man! as all i think when i look at them
i wouldn't want to spend one single solitary
second with one of them and can't stand
anyone who may be admired or looked up
to or referred to as something of a self-made man.

For stein, gertrude

don't tell me i can't pick my nose by the portrait of the picked fruit
while i choose to pick my nose by the portrait of the picked fruit
who said i can't pick my nose by the portrait of the picked fruit
i will pick my nose if i want to by the portrait of the picked fruit
i feel like one of those old black & white yiddish silent films
being censored & muted & you always get to play the role
of saint & martyr & of course i'm the victim & the bad
father picking my nose by the portrait of the picked fruit
marriage is a prison where the wife is a warden & need
to find my fiddle & middle ground on the roof on the
boardwalk by the portrait of the picked fruit. where
are those sheep that simply come waltzing in in
those watercolors in those pictures from the shtetl
in this bread & butter life sentence & we all go down & die
on the distant horizon right by the portrait of the picked fruit.

```
Addendum: on the lifelong life
of g. stein & alice b. toklas
```

I.

on self-
deprivation,
celebration
(same as self-
mutilation &
self-preservation)
or how to prepare
to prepare
to prepare
to cook a goose
with your down
time way after
the holidays
on a fine raw
drizzly over-
cast day
not too far
from monmartre
when you finally
feel comfortable
in your own
smock
like jambon
et fromage
croissants
pouffing
hair & doing
her makeup
in her switch
blade jack
knife fine
ally content
being an ex-
patriot with
4 chiens

named after
the surrealists
& french
symbolists
with a ticket
in the back
pocket of
yer apron
for gare
de lyon
& thee
south of france
knowing all
the twists
& turns
& palm
trees
by
heart

II.

italy.
friday.
don't respond
s'il-vous plait.
how much
for the ballet?
the chalet
on the lake?
that one much
closer to thee
dusk-dawn
of heaven
when look
king from
the train
window
coming
frum venice

where those
old men hold
up traffic
with their
mob of sheep
as opposed
to those
little bo
peeping
wannabe
aristocrats
whose silly
little seething
just feels
obvious
& repetitive
cruel
& cheap
& might
be nice
to have
access
to row
boats
&
kind
women
in sun
dresses
whose
small
talk
keeps
you
afloat

III.

when you
were young

she was so
young she
used to take
her stuffed
animal
with her
every
where
we went
as some
transitional-
object (d'art)
every place
we traveled
all over
europe
venice,
lake lugana,
emerald isle,
nice,
santorini,
sevilla,
sicilia,
valencia,
barcelona
& used
to get a
kick out
of how all
the young
housekeepers
sometimes
seductive
sisters
who felt
even younger
would place
& prop it up
in different parts
of our hotel room

IV.

the fact is before
you were ready
to finally take off
to your long-lost
gypsy vagabond
haunts in portugal
most specifically
the azures
had to figure
out what to do
with that sky-
blue mandolin
you had purchased
from that pharmacy
window in washington
heights, manhattan
triggering sweltering
summer evenings
& remembrances
of cloisters
contemplative
strolls over
the george
washington
& the brilliant
mists of
the hudson
so it wasn't
even so much
missing any
specific human
but most of all
what to do
with that
sky-blue
mandolin
from that
pharmacy
window

which
never
let you
down
& kept
you from
feeling
blue

V.

on blue
gloom
& doom
days you
take time
out to spit
shine thee
furniture &
hope the
deer &
ante
lope
are
doing
fine
& sir
viving
thee
wintry
season

VI.

when thee
snows calm
down might
as well
be thee

lower
east
side
might
as well
might
be A
bodega
& see
ing eye
dog a-
long thee
tinkling
wind-
chime
East
river
might
as well
be an ole
polish
widow
brooding
in her moo
moo might
as well
might
as well
might
as well
finally
be right
over might
those long
sighing fog
horns right
up along thee
hudson inn
side sleepy
holler wit
nothing

& every
thing
to look for
ward to

VII.

look back
wards too
to all those
model glue
airplane
instructions
encyclopedias
sports statistics
manuals of
etiquette
suburban
yellow
pages
where
would
call up
bridal shops
& ask them
to marry me
in my child
hood voice
of mockery
& hear these
young ladies
giggling (prob
ably the exact
same i'd see
naked in
the ladies
lockeroom
when my
mom
would

take me
swimming
at the y)
thee alice
b. toklas
cookbook
boxcar diner
menus &
chinese
menus
which
read
like the
egyptian
& tibetan
book of
the dead
how to
conjugate
irregular
verbs which
led absolutely
nowhere &
would only
use until
decades
later on-
the-run
frum
amerika

VIII.

when all
my report
cards read
was a class
clown with
great potential
didn't know

how to
take that
took that for
a compliment
& questioned
potential for
what matter
of fact even
felt resent
full while
perhaps
in my
hard
of hearts
felt they
were
sexually-
repressed
& passive-
aggressive
& just did
end get it
& had mad
heart & spirit
& really sin
searly was
contributing
something
positive to
the environ
meant thee
only way i
knew how in
the true-blue
ambiance
of thar
here
& now

IX.

child
hood
wuz
the
con-
fusion
between
suicide
notes &
love letters
nodding-out
in the class-
room & upon
awakening
not sure if
out of just
anger
or anxiety
folding it
into the
perfect
paper
airplane
& tossing
it out the
window in-
to the bleak
change of
seasons

X.

in retro
spec
when
it came
down to
it i got

deceived
by all the
people they
referred to
as honest
(the mean
& wicked
typewriting teacher
the old hag french
professor just
hanging around
to collect pension
the punitive principal
& his best friend
gym teacher)
when it came
down to it why
i had to go it alone
when it came
down to it
why i turned
towards the
companionship
arms & bosoms
of one-night stand
long-lost girlfriends
& gained all my
wisdom & rev-
elations in thee
rhythm
of pill-
low talk

XI.

my first love
was a very
removed
cousin
who i

had
heard
had a
mad
crush
on me
from
3,000
miles
away
out in
kalifornia
& decided
to just become
pen pals & first
she would just
end it with hugs
& kisses until
in the end it
all ended up
looking like
some hard
core score
card of xx
oooxxooxx

XII.

that girl
from yeshiva
university wurz
weiler school of
social work who
got pissed at her
best friend from
the island for outing
her as being a republican
but actually was a real-
life nymphomaniac &
in the middle of class

confessed to me she
was wearing no under
wear & what was
i supposed to do
with that follow
up with some
real clever
fine pithy
punchline
like prove
it or meet
me in the
bathroom
anywhich
way it'd
all end up
sleazy &
you'd end
up guilty
asking her
to leave
social
policy
to relieve
all stressors
& tensions
when was
just simply
following
up with
her offer
ending up
poverty-
stricken
on pro-
bation?

XIII.

claiming the best one
can do which seems
something of a lame
leftover proverb is
to live something
of a happy &
healthy life
got no idea
what that
would look
like...like
the closest i
ever got was
my beating
heart waiting
for the plane
to take off
from la
guardia
to charles
der gawl
with a couple
bucks in my
pocket knowing
all the things
i was gonna
do when i got picked
up by that little mad
man dwarf taxidriver
snapping his fingers
to some really
strange out
dated disco
i guess digging it
cuz thought i was
something of a hipster
wired wasted gangster
from amerika whizzing
with tears in my eyes

sentimental reflective
past le tour d'eiffel
driving & winding
wild up the cobble
stone hills of mon
martre just like
g. stein &
alice b.
toklas

XIV.

a rose
by any
other
name
be pink
in a white vase
like those beautiful
scarred red brick
row of gorgeous
monochromatic
buildings on
23rd street
across from
the infamous
chelsea a little
further down
towards 8th
& 9th avenue
on the westside
when the sun
hits it just
right right
around
twilight
going
down
over the
palisades

in jersey
where
they
keep
the holy
flowing
hudson
streaming
vast & open
transcendently
leaving room open
for the imagination

XV.

all those symbolic
archetypal myth
ological dream
like beasts &
animals which
now just co
habitate &
physically
show up to
your window
what if in (f)act
without even
being aware
of it have done
something of
a role-reversal
touching on the
notion in your
later stages
of growth &
development
have become
them in mind
body spirit
& soul

solitary
contemplative
with a heart
of gold always
having a little
fear of yourself
& deep down inside
knowing your some
thing of a primal
gentle giant
as well

XVI.

how to
live alone
how to
listen to
classical
radio
french
rap &
staticky
jazz
from
n'orleans
how to
make
petite
fois
faux
gras
& a
new
sense
of yer
self
at thee
chinese
rest

o-rant
how
to eat
a pear
dipped
inn A
kettle
of
car-
amel
when
yer
all
by
yer
lone
some
by a
map
filled
out on
your kit
chin island
by your child
of the united
states of
amerika.

```
for Nietzsche, Friedrich:
an ancient hx of the contemporary world
```

i want to create my own language of words without definitions
of simply beat and rhythm deriving overall meaning from
the context of fluidity and the state of flux of being

aphorism: a miracle would be a democrat and republican
sitting in an empty room together in the middle of *the
naked city* and one appearing in deep thought with
eyes shut responding "i never thought of it that way"

theme from: "it came from outer space"

the opaque light which creeps over the pyramids
over the bronx over reno nevada over the boxcar
diner over the dinner theater over the dog races
over karaoke over the acropolis over the coliseum

excerpt from pain diary: i love when they don't
take me seriously and constantly scapegoat me
(the obvious nit-wits that they are) as inspires
me to write love sonnets and blow them away
like an ancient egyptian on his deathbed getting
ready for the final farewell stage of reincarnation

the ability to dream is to realize your nightmares

god is a deck of playing cards...

george carlin declared: "the forecast for tonight will be dark"

what went terribly wrong with america
is everywhere you turn (every channel
you turn) is some late-night host; good
when you just solely had johnny carson
with that million-dollar smile not
too far from carson city, nevada

surviving off fresh-squeezed orange juice
breakfast burritos and marijuana

humor from the little rascals: the mr. hood one–
"i have a headache in my stomach!" mr. hood responds
manically muttering to himself "a headache in my stomach…"

those who made the blacklist or ostracized in some form or
another: lenny bruce, charlie chaplin, jack kerouac, jim morrison
as it really wasn't so much them but the 'absurd' system which
they lived in (refer to paul goodman) that simply became uptight
and rigid (like almost every closed-minded insular community
in america) and no longer receptive like the rumors and
routines and rituals of religion

these are real people and not actors: i beg to differ…

Waking Up Dead Alone In One Of Those Gigantic Champagne Glasses Full Of Bubbles

Every morning I am awoken by a big black crow
just sitting perched on a branch outside my window
gazing through the mist to the mountain as if planning
for his day then swoops down and vanishes. When I used to
live out in Coney Island, Brooklyn at the end of the boardwalk
which felt like the last home in the world all by my lonesome
I used to love to watch great flocks of docile seagulls gather
and line up in rows like a ceremony on shore watching some
great ball of fire gradually go down dip down and disappear
on the distant horizon as if they somehow deep-down inside
intuitively knew trying to figure out the ways of the world
brooding and reflecting and paying respect and homage
about what the previous day had brought them and felt
was always able to relate to them so much more and
did relate to them so much more on the most subtle
and deepest of sensory levels, as opposed to that
awful, erratic, predictable lot of humans who
seemed so much more (wrong and disloyal)
mean-spirited and impulsive, exhibiting specific
behavioral patterns of constantly "going in for the kill."

When the sun finally did disappear I'd hear them
just naturally, suddenly, start to weep and wail in
unison lifting their skulls and wings to the heavens
like brilliant, histrionic mourners which seemed
to really make the most sense of all and
get down deep in one's heart and soul.

A Natural Phenomenological History Of Planting

Alas, I cut out the fields at dusk, and in the first patch, it is going to be pumpkins in the first row, the 200 lbs. ones, then the 100 lbs. ones and then the ones you bake the pies with, and the last row set for the squash and zucchini. In the next patch will be the sweet corn whose line echoes the natural curve of the woods and had to plant three rows for purposes of cross-breeding and survival and the final patch is reserved for the sunflowers, which will hopefully grow long and narrow, flush against the silvery, metallic barn as the first row is for the small and the last the large, and got mentioned the latter has a tendency to get oily so watch out for bear coming down from the mountains and will keep an eye out. It also was observed in a couple of them, slugs, so rec- ommended to leave out some cans of cheap beer, as supposedly they are naturally attracted to their scent so I guess will have to relive my youth of underage drinking, watching them do kamikaze dives and missions into cans of *Old Milwaukee*, and eventually, in the long-run, it will all be honky-dory so I guess all that's left to do now, and something of a waiting game like some stray wild turkey spending his day perched, brooding on top a telephone pole, eavesdropping on other people's rapport to look out for the corn and pumpkins and sunflowers to grow.

    Dear Protocol...

in the beginning of the dark night
you hear a loud thud outside
the window of your home.
you know what it is but
don't want to admit it.
cars start to slow down
to a crawl and gather around
while wife says the poor soul
is struggling trying to get back up.
you tell her she better call the cops.
you ask her what do they do now
and is there anything they can do
to help him out like can they try and
bring him to an animal hospital or veterinarian?
you tell her you don't know why you always
feel far worse if an animal gets hit than a human
that just 15 minutes ago he was alive and kicking
and imagine my spirit in him and can he even
begin to comprehend what is happening
solitary stranded struggling and suffering?
the woman over the phone says there's nothing they
can do and all they can do is put it out of its misery.
a cop with a flashing beamer in the middle
of the deep dark evening shows up
while all you hear is one gun shot.
wife sees cop simply drag carcass off
and drop him off right in front of our home.
no ringing of doorbell.
no giving us a call.
you tell her to call back the cops and they tell
us they won't be back tonight. some time
tomorrow morning the game warden
will come by to pick him up.
we are repulsed.
repulsed that no one stopped by.
repulsed no one gave us a call.
repulsed no one seems to give a damn
about the stirring spirit of this poor soul
and all they seem to care about is protocol.

she tells them we have
a young son and can
they please have someone
come by to pick him up
as we don't want him to see him
before driving to school tomorrow.
what about the wild dogs?
what about the coyote?
what about the crows?
they say she will have to
call the regular number.
they are just as cold.
we are on our own.
we call up an acquaintance
we know who happens
to hunt and appears
very eager and excited.
he shows up right away
and rings our doorbell
and asks us if later on
we will want venison.
wife says no and all
we are both thinking
of is the wandering
soul of this poor creature.
he tells us to call back the cops
and that will be picking him up.
they very coldly tell us he can't
and that that's not protocol
and will have to wait
until the game warden.
she hangs up the phone
and you tell her fuck them.
did they give a damn
when they just dropped
him off in front of our home
while the poor soul has already been
dragged and removed from the shoulder?
we can feel his lingering spirit. something
we felt since the original thud stirring
and swirling up into heaven...

Not In The Job Description

My grandmother used to literally pick up
the winos from The Bowery and haul them up
to her summer camp for the summer who used to
always have these very long and dramatic profound
names named after such leaders like Nathaniel Hawthorne
...Benjamin Franklin...Woodrow...and interestingly made
pretty good cooks always in those tight undershirts with
a pack of *Pall-Malls* tucked underneath right around the shoulders
where they kept their smudged, faded, merchant marine tattoos
usually involving some sort of anchor or voluptuous naked girl
and used to be pretty good and decent workers and do pretty
well all until they had those nights off and nights on the town
then turn into real-life Dr. Jekyll and Mr. Hydes and literally
have to try and find and locate them on do or die missions
somewhere in the middle of the mountains, the rabid
alcoholics that they were and head into town with
the senior counselors to see if they might be able
to track them down riding up and down route 7
in The Berkshires to all the local barrooms and have
to drag them out I swear sometimes by the elbows
sometimes by the ankles into the sandy parking lot
while they'd holler such stuff out loud about the hippies
or government in the back of her racing gold Cadillac
taking off through the swamps and stars while slurring
and singing all the old great romantic crooners cruising
back to the silhouetted bunks on the lake in the forest
where they'd sleep it off and conveniently forget it all
after their infamous and classic blackouts. They all died
pretty young and tragic though and was always some
sort of folklore attached to them like real-life slapstick
comedians slipping on banana peels and tumbling
down the stairs of the subway and suffering from
internal bleeding found dead in Tinpan Alley not
coincidentally too far off from The Bowery...

It still did prove to be pretty shocking
as in many ways did become family
and an extension to her being
and had made some sort of

serious sincere connection
as strange as that may seem.

Just A Little Higher Than Higher Education

The substitute teachers we always liked more and had crushes
on with a good sense of humor eating warm muenster cheese
sandwiches in the teacher's lounge and were young and romantic
and had good sex lives. We always liked them so much more than
the regular teachers who didn't seem as involved or do their jobs
as well and always out on maternity leave or sick leave or having
something else to do with that awful sorority of unionized
things with their degrees in bullshitting and very mean and
punitive and Dickensian things. Wolves wander down the hall
with a powdering of snow in their fur coats and those slight grins
on somewhere between lunch and wood shop where the beautiful
tomboy gangsta' girls are always smirking and flirting with wise ass
delinquent boys both in goggles and both getting themselves into
a hell of a lot of trouble but don't give a shit for good reason and
charming and noble and simply extensions of troubled households
getting so much more out of life and so much more sincere and
substantial than any of those goody-goodies and good deed
doers and perfectly organized and blindly following the rules
and I guess what they call driven so they can just get themselves
into good colleges and be schmucks of civilization. All the single
mothers with their seething scowls wait for their little angels at
pick-up while the young good looking fathers simply minding
their own business representative of all the guys who cheated
on them become scapegoats and it's like the school dance all
over again standing on opposite sides of the gym. The sign in
the schoolyard reminds us of the sleigh rules and what to do
with our sleds when it starts to come down during the season.

```
Ghosts
```

Where does the crossing guard go when she's good and gone
gone home and vanishes into thin air almost like the opposite
of our (or Descarte's proof or non-proof) belief in God based
on know he's there or exists because every time I think of him
I can just feel it; get so sick of it out here in this here United
States of America how we're so obsessed and care so much
about how a president's gonna get rated or judged or when
we look back at him and his legacy (I mean can we really
objectify or compare Abraham Lincoln to Woodrow Wilson
to Theodore Roosevelt to John F. Kennedy?) as opposed to
what they really do (or sincerely try to do) when in desperate
need and feeling collectively blue (yeah I'd call that something
of a great depression) sort of like that old cliche of "a friend
in need is a friend indeed" so getting back to the notion
and image (religion or non-religion) of what happens
to the crossing guard when she's good and gone
and gone home and vanishes into thin air
or our or Descarte's belief in God

There are just some mathematical equations
in my opinion better left unsaid and unsolved.

That Fleeting Forgotten Period

I suppose the one good thing about being a teenager
was the literal and physical and geometric positions
one would assume philosophizing with best friends
and acquaintances under dining room tables
first highs at keg parties with fine buzzes
and intoxications no feeling like it feeling
no pain walking on cloud nine working
the room with quick and clever schmoozes
and punch lines wrestling rivals in front yards
under floodlights in midnight autumnal leaf piles
dirty dancing dry-fucking girls you had crushes on
and finding out they actually had secret crushes on
you and it all coming to a head all cumming true right
there and then in the moment feeling those erogenous
zones and erotic parts and shapes and contours of
the body like some fantasy come alive in the family
playroom waking up literally not knowing where
you were disoriented boozed-up either in guest
bathrooms with your head literally *hung over*
the toilet or right there on the floor where you last
dropped your bones beside sofas not even making
it up there to the cushions and pillows on top of
appliances on top of washers and dryers cuz
the only space left as the rest of the house
taken over by drunken friends while single
divorced fathers showed up from the city
like some battlefield in the morning with
all those passed-out strewn bodies because
it was their weekend to take the kid and you
keeping them charmed and laughing able to
really dig and escape and relate to your reality.

That Phase Which Never Gets Mentioned

I miss and recollect being a wise ass and derelict
way back in the day back in the halls of high school
all of us having the exact same novels tucked under
our elbows with our notebooks and folders and was
always so fucked-up and shallow the ones who were
the most organized and driven considered the smartest
but in retrospect how many loopholes and contradictions
to that reasoning and equation yet remembering all those
same classic novels The Catcher In The Rye by Salinger 1984
by Orwell A Brave New World and On The Road by Kerouac
The Metamorphosis by Kafka all with the same sort of simple
and spare classy monochromatic covers usually of a cranberry
or gold and boy if these brilliant and tortured souls only knew
and saw and could see this image played out in the heart
of suburbia all those jocks and jerks and perverts and
cheerleaders carrying them around with them from class
to class bell to bell like some forgotten sort of mandated
adolescent bible kind of the whole irony and tragedy and
punchline and theater of the absurd of it all like a cross
between the symbolic and literal (without even knowing it)
which made it all that much more surreal from Kafka to
Kerouac to Salinger to Orwell and recall having a solid
b+ average and being bored out of my skull...

Home Economics

Who was that cliched idiot
who came up with all that shit
when you cheat you're just cheating
yourself as for me never felt more alive
or got more of an adrenalin rush or sense
of pride and self (respect) independence
and accomplishment and achievement
from all those smug motherfuckers
who had fed me all that brainwash
and bullshit and kept me down
for so damn long and ironically
resulted in feeling nothing
at all no sense of pride
or self so when i acted
out which i pretty much
had no choice in the matter
and cheated and got
away with it perversely
felt so much more a part of
and substantial and a sense
of belonging and holy (from
the phony-boloney holy-moly
higher-than-holy) connected
to my culture and psychosocial
environment on practically every
strata and every level and feeling down
to earth rather than down in the dumps
disconnected and disempowered and
possession of the pawn of the devil.

Hypnosis

In the early days of high school I used to have this friend
of mine and with our free time or guess what they refer to
downtime having nothing better to do than sit in his kitchen
at night during the weekend and try to hypnotize each other
putting each other under some spell saying such self-soothing
and suggestive shit like "imagine you're in the middle of a sea
and it's just simply rolling and you can hear the waves rippling
being carried away being pulled away by a million balloons"
then would like snap his fingers and make me try to push
his refrigerator with my shoulder grunting and groaning
and that's how we'd spend our weekends like a bunch
of teenage linebackers moaning and groaning trying
to push his refrigerator from one end of the kitchen
to the other; his parents were divorced like most
of them were and he lived with his father who
was never around and just saw his grandmother
who was this pretty nice old lady and would always
have these decorative dishes set up in the foyer or living
room always replenished with *Hershey's* chocolate kisses
and survived off *Chef Boyardee* spaghetti and meatballs and
think it would be pretty cool these days to just fill up dishes
around my home with different sorts of medications and drugs
like opiates and opium and morphine and speed for whenever
I'm feeling down in the dumps down on my luck and would
take one every so often and self-medicating myself with this
controlled substance in a controlled manner (like those Kisses
and can of Chef Boyardee) actually providing a real pleasant
and sentimental trigger and bringing me back to those days
and think man what in the hell would be so wrong with that?

Scenes From Inside The Origami Bomb

I remember a good buddy of mine
caught us all off guard and by surprise
and couldn't believe had the nerve to do it
and apparently had been living something
of a second or even a third life and had a
scholarship to one of the best engineering
colleges in America, never knew he had an
addiction to painkillers held up some schmaltzy
suburban pharmacy with a clear mask over
his face somewhere in his senior year around
rush hour during a rather gloomy hour before
they had one of those mood disorders which
had something to do with light deprivation
or depression from the weather. Well recently
been developing a hankering and wondering
if anyone ever held up a *Food Emporium*
for their lox and *Temp-tee* cream cheese;
a New York tradition and delicacy. Don't think
I'd have the nerve to do it with the mischievous
impulsivity and poor judgment only teenagers
seem capable of during that opaque anxious
period somewhere between high school and
college. Remember at the time, them saying
that one crazy move pretty much screwed-up
and fucked-up his life for good and strangely
enough myself experiencing the perverse emotional
phenomenon and not sure why maybe because I was
fascinated he was the silent type or really envied him
perhaps because at the time likewise was bombarded
and overwhelmed as well by an overbearing authority
figure who constantly felt the compulsive need to put
me on trial and lecture me about pseudo-morality and
responsibility and maybe subconsciously felt like some
proverbial desperate escape to freedom and the classic
rebellion and really looked up to him for having the balls
to do it or felt a certain amount of liberation or kinship
and wondering recently in the here and now what's
become of him and how the heck he is doing?

He had a good heart and probably putting up cities...

The Colonel's Best

Funny whenever I used to
get into trouble as a kid and
literally have my day in court
after would visit the drive-thru
at *Kentucky Fried Chicken*
(almost became something
of a tradition Pavlov's dog
trigger and even developed
a fine rapport and relationship
with all the cute girls at the window
which think somehow influenced
my taste and interests for them
in the future) and pick up a
bucket of The Colonel's Best
along with sides and usually by
the size of the bucket and every-
thing else in the bag my family
could pretty much figure out
my fate and how I did and it
was all so damn dysfunctional
back then seeming to thrive off
all that guilt and shame and drama
and damage and acting-out totally
unaware of it in a maddening yet
scrumptious vicious cycle from
an awfully hypercritical and
subjugating authority figure.

Chomping on a piece of extra-crispy
on my way home from the court-
house became my freedom.

```
Walmart
```

One day the whole
world's gonna just
explode and
gonna all be
i mean we're
all gonna be
on a big
flatscreen tv
all perfectly
prepackaged
and wrapped
up in a box
sticking out
of a shopping
cart pushed by
a big piece of
white trash
at *walmart.*

The Lack Of Influence Of Media On The Lacking Individual

I want to meet my love
on christian mingle.com
and wonder what those
first dates will be like?
are you only allowed
to talk about all things
christian? do you only
have christian friends
who likewise only like
to mingle with christ?
do you look into each
other's eyes and tell
each other how you
just want to raise your
kids christian and fall
head over heels for each
other and do that little cute
twirly-whirly safe disco dance
and only move to all christian
dead ends? and right when
we're walking down the aisle
with all our christian friends
and family adoringly staring
straight at us i'll break the news
to her and whisper in her ear–
"i'm jewish will that be alright?"
probably be like the closing scene
from "the graduate" where they're
both running away from those old
farts in the cathedral and they
put the crucifix in the lock
just to get away from them
but this time might be
without the bride.

That Pretty Poor Girl From Illinois

You ever get a girl's face in your mind
you can't get out however hard you try?
well that happened tonight. it was this
really young beautiful red head with those
great big blue eyes and great behind well more like
a lot of junk in her trunk and i'm like damn what
the fuck? where do i know her from? social work
school back at yeshiva? from internship? or am
i so fucked-up and reached that phase where
i forgot and actually used to date her? then
suddenly it hit me was some friend from
facebook from way back in the day
think she was a poor girl or so she
claimed or grew up that way and
lived in illinois and think used to
work at like *old navy* and would
always take pictures of herself
like holding cups of *starbucks*
as if this would make her look
more classy and cultured and
would even take selfies of her
in her small single-white female
apartment of her in her cut-off
blue jeans with those great big
blue eyes and pouty lips and of
course all that junk in her trunk
and pose all those obvious and
seductive and rhetorical questions
begging for an answer and fishing
for compliments from her very safe
and secure playing possum distance
like don't i look good? and always
just kind of change her hairstyle
as though it would somehow
make her life seem worthwhile
but still looked just as sad and lost
and wild always with the same kind
of drama and deep down inside kind
of felt there was no guy who was ever

quite right for her or she was too good
for them and so on and used to
try to help her out with older
man advice when she found
herself in a pickle or was in
crisis and would write
some of the most boring
and predictable shit back
and even found myself
a bit pissed by that
and then thought
this ain't worth it
and why in the heck
am i even writing to
this girl from illinois
who i don't even know
but then looking back
obviously know
exactly why.

Well however she turned out
do hope she found the right guy...

```
Need That As Much As I Need A Head In The Hole
```

Always got freaked out
by girls who suddenly
felt the need to confess
their feelings for me
like why and how
in the hell could they
possibly have feelings
for me like they actually
took the time out to think
they had feelings for me
as i had no feelings for
me and even at times
became this emotional
trigger for some strange mixture
of resentment and self-loathing
and what would they now want
and expect from me and what
did they want me to say to such
things like o yeah? like some
awkward absurd punchline
at the end of some comic
tragedy like are you kidding
but then when i actually got
to thinking about it thought
man pretty damn neat
and why in the hell
not me and what
took them (or me)
so long like some
really strange surreal
moment in time like
citizen kane's snow
globe suddenly
falling tumbling
and crashing
to the dust
and grime
cracking
and me

something between cracking and cracking
up and being all that ooze oozing out
from the nostalgic sentimental seasons
(having repressed after years and years
of blocking and not even knowing it)
and the past and present and future
all coming together through the scar
tissue and damage finally realizing
while simultaneously suddenly
forgetting which in essence
is the most cool and keen
is the greatest discovery.

Somewhere Around Yonkers

Growing up in a Jewish family
on Sunday evening (always felt
for some reason during the seasons
of Autumn or Winter when it got dark
earlier) like some real telepathic shit
like–"You will get Chinese...You
will get Chinese..." and the hard-to-get
playing possum routine passed down
from generation to generation of who
heads over to the drawer flowing over
with all those menus which you could
barely open reciting all the different
options and combinations studying
it and analyzing it and debating and
brainstorming and breaking it down
on every different level from every
different perspective (what the
famous psychologists like to
refer to as the very keen and lucid
of the olfactory senses and what
would be the payoff and what
would be the consequences)
putting little checks next to
the boneless spareribs and
crab rangoon usually some
sort of shrimp and sweet
and sour and do we or do
we not want to get rice or
noodles and the chosen one
of who would go out into the deep
dark dusk through the towns over
the border to pick it up then plop
it right next to you in the passenger
seat all warm and piping and pungent
like some long-lost friend or companion
some girlfriend who'll never leave you
some babushka straight from the shtetl
with that classic rock and roll station
always serenading you in the background

the soundtrack to your adolescence to like
Led Zeppelin or Van Halen or Eric Clapton
and returning home with that big bag
flowing over like some pot of gold
at the end of the rainbow all heroic
and humble feening like Pavlov's dog
having killed Pavlov (fuck him!)
and breaking open the seltzer

Denouement in the end
always repeated over
and over again like
some half-crazed
routine or ritual
or tradition
dramatically
declared by
your mother–
"I'm stuffed!
Never eating
Chinese again."

It's A Story...

Jan gets up in the middle of the night
about 3 am from that tiny ticking
Zenith alarm clock she's got set
aside right by her bedside
while perfectly planned
precise pulls the knife
out from beneath her
Mickey Mouse pillow.
Cindy strategically
sleeps with one eye open
as already onto her and
knows things about her
that would completely
freak people out and
blow their mind and
forced to become
smart and streetwise.
Jan stealthily slips on
her fuzzy pink slippers
and her pink terrycloth
robe and slowly secretly steps
over exaggerated and full of gusto
like a caricature imitating her favorite
television detectives and while Marsha
is deep in slumber with a great big grin
dreaming of the boyfriends and siblings
she has taken advantage of and sadistically
tortured Jan finds the perfect moment
in time to suddenly lunge and tug
and pull at her long glistening mane
of blonde hair brushed 100 times
puts the Swiss Army Knife right
to her lily-white neck and with
eyes psychotically flashing, glowing
almost cross-eyed, whispers kind
of Clint Eastwood-like–"Just so
you know I can get you anytime,
anytime of day, anytime of night"
as Marsha just lies there petrified

shaking and shuttering, finally modest
and humble, admitting–"I got it, I got it"
while Jan moves back across the shag
carpet for the first time experiencing
that thing they call self-esteem at last
completely satisfied and contented
taking off those pink fuzzy slippers
that pink terrycloth robe; puts
the sleeping mask back over her
eyes and gets the best beauty sleep
she's gotten her whole entire life
and like children like devils like angels
wake up and get out of bed as if nothing
had ever happened; Mike and his wife
having spent the night doing it multiple
times in a variety of different positions
somewhere between that freak Alice
and her bondage and Parent Teacher's
Association, while the boys touching
and fondling and getting familiar with
themselves, some of them jerking-off
and Zen-Buddhist like neither looking
back to the past or looking forward
to the future live in the moment and
let it all go right below those Cowboy
and Indian sheets and blankets feeling
no guilt or conflict cuz they're not exactly
quite related, stepsisters through another
marriage, blended of the blonde mixture
and when it all really comes down
to it, something of a mirage.

Denouement:

Everything emanates from the deep
warm moist swamp of the suburbs
in the Technicolor tincture of lawns
and lovers somewhere in the middle
between the idealism of the late Sixties
and bizarre reality of the early Seventies.

Guest Villain

My kid this morning
showed up from his
room with a popsicle
stick with writing on
it and said–"daddy
i just couldn't tell
you so i had to
write it" and asked
"dylan please tell me"
and he flipped it over
and it simply read
"they shot archie!"
while apparently
the motherfucken
losers and cowards
of the day the only
way they could think of
ending it all for the last
and final comic book
was to kill off archie
from archie comics
someone we grew up
with and forever embedded
in our imagination and consciousness
and that's all they could come up with
like what the fuck? have him whacked
or *ended* or get caught in the crossfire
and used to really like that section of
the bronx in riverdale where i used
to date a lot of cute and crazy jewish
girls and met my betrothed and whose
experience would not trade for all
the tea in china or rugelach at
gruenebaum's and *mother's*
and suppose nothing like
betty or vernonica but
really not terribly far.

What's In A Name?

Wife told me after one of our son's
friends out of nowhere just jumped
in her car after school and declared
he was hungry, as she uses the gift
certificates her mom from the bronx
always sends her for places like
mcdonald's while another younger
sister of my son's friends jumped
in as well and with all their crazy
cross talk right by them was stopped
mr. softee with the words written under
his window ding-a-ling and they exclaimed
"there's mr. ding-a-ling!" who supposedly
has a bit of a reputation in the neighbor
hood of being something of a pervert
only to discover when they got there
they stopped having old men dressed
up as ronald mcdonald for the exact same
reason now dressed as dogs how you figure?

Only Red White And Blue I Ever Worshiped

Tonight Erica suddenly
flipped her head like
a domestic Scarlet O'hara
in the middle of the steps
and went–"Why don't you
clean the lint!" I was drinking
a rum & coke feeling no pain
while watching old episodes
of *Wonder Woman* with the
sound turned off as everything
back then seemed like a cross
between a beauty pageant
and Dick Van Patten, some
secret espionage mission
rope suddenly being cut
from way up above to drop
a light (and end the life...)
from atop the stage to fall
right on top of some starlet
in sequins to end it all; you
look forward to those days
when you may sit in one
of those electric chairs
going up and down
your staircase with
a mixed drink
reminiscing
your boyhood
wondering when
Lynda Carter and
Suzanne Somers
would just stay
still long enough
for you to get
your rocks off
and when that
torpedo suddenly
shot off it was
as if that truth

lasso had been
tossed and squeezed
out all conflicts and
crises of existence
and like some
miracle just
forget it all
with instant
forgiveness
as if nothing
in the world
had ever existed
and this elevated
state of stimulation
of emptiness and
nothingness strangely
enough seemed like
something quite
noble to shoot for
or for that matter
not to shoot for.

Clint Eastwood

After one of those insane
                power-struggles
                      with the wife
  when you prove
      yourself right
           (not really looking to
                    but know you're
                        not wrong
          and the exact opposite of
what she's accusing you of)
          by every possible
      mode & means
    of communication
        & clarification
  & logical point
    of debate
      & argumentation
    they still never once
  mention they are wrong
enough to put
      a gun to the head
  & always hit you
like on
    thanksgiving
      or new year's
          as there's a reason
  why they gave us clint eastwood
          with his 357 magnum
              to lose yourself
        in your easy chair
  who always manages
      to get all the pretty
          1970's milfs
            with the sandy
              windswept
                blonde hair
in the fishy psychotic town
        of san francisco

                              where there are
                         always
                    blue skies
               looking out
                    from the bell
                         bottom
                                   windchime
                              sagebrush
                    kite-flying cliffs
          to the foghorns
                    of the pacific
     to good ol'
          cathartic
               chickenwire
                    alcatraz
                         giving you time
                              to be reflective
                                   & make sense of it all
                         in the fucken
                              sociopathic
                                   madness of it all
                    there was also steve mcqueen
          that blonde bombshell
& michael & jj evans
               who helped you escape
                         in the chainsnatching
                                   do-or-die projects
                                             of chicago
where is our clint eastwood
               steve mcqueen
                    & kid dyn-o-mite!
                              from chi-town?
     you turn to the leftover
               fried chicken
                    & rum & coke
                         on the counter
     that last scene
          from "escape from alcatraz"
                    where that flower
                         is discovered
                                   on devil's island…

Moving On Up But Not Quite Exactly

Woke up this morning to George
engaged in a power-struggle
going face to face, toe to toe
with that jive-talking house-
keeper of his, who always
refuses to clean his moving-
on-up apartment; for some
strange reason I found it
hilarious and cracking-up
and really able to somehow
relate to it; my wife told me
she couldn't watch it cause he
reminded him too much of her
father another jive-talker but
Jewish and a banker and used
to always cheat on her mother,
as other husbands would just
show up to their door in The
Bronx and threaten to kill him;
they used to leave messages over
their answering machine of "Staying
Alive" and now lives the good life
somewhere down in The Sunshine
State with his second wife, the last
woman he cheated on her mom with
and now acts like the shit cuz no longer
Reformed, but one step higher on the
proverbial ladder of success as converted
to a Conservative...How you figure?
Even lived a brief stint with The Indian
from The Village People who looked more
Puerto Rican than anything Native-American
like Juan Epstein from *Welcome Back Kotter*
in The Riverdale Section of The Bronx
where Archie & Veronica got their start

Any which way
looking back
I still liked

waking up
to George
and that
housekeeper
of his going at it.

That Missing Piece To The Puzzle

The anti-Christ traipsing through *Home Depot*
with his fluorescent halo right around that part
of The West Coast they're getting all that global
warming and the sediment of muddy copper
rivers overflowing in Utah leaving sepia
photos of polygamist sects, 7 wives just
standing there sexless, traumatized, like
a deer in headlights as if suddenly mater-
ialized and discovered in the ancient dust
dazed and distant with wooden expressions
in their pastel puritan *Scarlet Letter* dresses
somewhere in the middle of the half-crazed
baking desert between The Great Salt Lake
and Bryce Canyon Palm Springs California

(Hx Of Silent Movies:
all great porn started
from tiny pebbles
being thrown
at windows)

Heard back then in Hollywood everyone slept
with everyone; would have loved to have
smoked a blunt with Jimmy Dean with
everyone down on their luck like their
own version of denial and redemption.

Florida

      , soggy

New Orleans muggy maddening highest murder-rate per-capita
seems like that magnolia always stalking you to empty haunted
midnight streets of mobile, alabama after getting blasted with
a bunch of southern belles from the catholic university heading
beneath the stars to the gulf to biloxi to go splashing naked silly

                                                mississippi...

In Apropos

why i must constantly shoot my load
cuz the world sucks and is horrible
and makes it all good and pure
and beautiful and bearable
i am not a criminal
i'm a mistaken identity
the first and last day out of prison
what are those? tulips? daffodils?
drifting in that aimless streetcar
as though through some portal
in time or sphere of emotions
not caring at all if i ever find my
way home through the magnolia
and crepe myrtle, as those rivers
which i grew up on and cohabited
and contemplated like the truckee
the winooski the bronx mississippi
will always historically spiritually
and transcendently be coursing
through my veins from bondage
and subjugation to slave freedom
to the blissful nowhere nothingness
of brilliant hollow void vacant as if
the world at last and all those
supposed humans in it
never existed; passes.

Tick-Tock Of Cats & Smokestacks

1, i want a home
    chock-full,
       overloaded,
          hoarded
      full of gorgeous
   subtle shapes
  & forms
of stained-glass
spheres, orbs
    hugging kitchen
        windows
          tinctured
      apothecarian
  mad scientist bottles
     lining the windowsills
          cluttered
     all over the shelves
   & coffee tables
shaking & clattering
    from dewy branches
         in the over-
    grown yard
  2, & when it comes
    beating,
      bleary-eyed
        during
          different
     times of the day
   radiating
 reflecting
   that brilliant
     refracted light
& shade of color
all over the place
in BLUES, reds, golds
violets, indigos, periwinkles
    3, you fading away
        self-soothed,
          silhouetted

by all things solitary
like that faithful intuitive
dog who lies sprawled
out on a daily basis,
                    sympathetic
(an opium addict)
            a regular in his
                        favorite spot
                                taking cat-naps
                        in the natural
                splendid warmth
        keeping an eye
out on the tchotckes
  4, your wife polishing
                the spoons you cook
                            down the dope in
                spit-shining
            the elvis,
     star wars,
first man on the moon
                    plates
                        glistening,
                            winking
                                    on the faded 1970's
        split-pea & golden, apocalyptic orange
striped menagerie wallpaper
        5, humanity should be more like
                        "the price is right"
                                with all those
                                        idiot
                                            heads
                                    bobbing madly,
                            hysterically
                        in unison
                    MUTED
                swaying,
                        swooning
                    everyone
        minding their own business
                    6, while you naturally dissolve
                                    in the poppy

                              poplars
                        tick of the clock
                     (taking-off
                  like an origami swan
                   to the ominous horizon)
           in scattered shadows
& colorful prisms
          during the stripped-
down skeleton change
of seasons.

Tally-Ho

i think i'd like to play cards
   with the wife all day
with a freshly picked
   out pack of cards
from *dollar general*
   opening them
      to the world
faded down on our luck
   nodding-out
on leftover morphine
      methadone
   manischewitz
medicine
   leftover
madmen
   realities
& phases
   used for just
the right occasion
   deciding
be just the right occasion
   be bleak sun
tumbling, bumbling
   gradually
bouncing off homemade
   terrariums
science experiments
   pre-pubescent
avocados & figures taking
   shelter inside
the shadowboxes
   not caring a wit
who wins or loses
   like rainy
day cardcastles
   as contentment
& satisfaction
   just about
the time put into it

   maybe a breeze
sweeping through window
   making it suddenly
blissfully fall on its own
   accord and that
in itself a revelation
   & this in itself
a vacation
   from fragile
& fucked-up existence
   no specific
build-up of weather wildfire
   ferries capsizing
people being taken hostage
   by the hostage-takers
& elections getting decided
   by the wealthiest
donors forecasting your future
   like perhaps one of
those old-time nostalgic sandcastle
   1950's radio station
buildings which somehow
   made it
ethereally, mystically
   through
the madness & mania
   through
the dusk & hush
   of switch-
blade seasons
   generations
& generations
   of thick & thin
of what is
   & what isn't.

Holding Your Breath Above Water

With all the chips stacked against me what other choice did I really
have but to build card castles in the breeze, while here there would
be no slaves or kings, no saviors or siblings, no thieves or success
stories, and my reality would only exist in the razor-thin fragility,
stacked precariously, somewhere between fate and coincidence and
irony between my nightmares and dreams, and when those idiot
cookie-cutter masses very casually, mechanically blasted through
their melancholy and drunken, lethargic loudspeakers, between the
metropolis and suburbs–"Land ho!" with rich girls passed-out
who had already put on their histrionic, decadent shows,
old men with mad smiles reminiscing disoriented, gazing from
fleeting windows, and that gigolo ticket taker always with a trick
up his sleeve, passionately able to relate to and believe, I just
naturally, instinctively, turned elsewhere towards the inner soul,
one of those token tourists they're always talking of, who suddenly
goes missing-in-action from one of those classic "Cruises of
a Lifetime" and conveniently never ever gets spoken of again
in polite conversation having nonchalantly, contented with pained
expression and *Dentyne* smile and "little dab will do you" jet-black
hair, simply vanished into thin air where the mad and the meek for
no rhyme or reason meet like criminals after confession exchanging
postcards of their arrested stages of development, and the only
thing they have in common is an uncommon language, disguises,
and a hell of a lot of damage in the slapstick madness of some
anarchist auditorium, cavorting amongst those drop-dead,
gorgeous, half-crazed mermaids who one day love you and the next
hate you, and fall in love with them for everything they have
learned not to believe in and all they no longer wish to be on those
ridiculous rough and tough, tumultuous seas having found my
solace and safety and security deep within the shallows of
anonymity, and everything they never taught me or at least
finally a place where they could never find me; my reality all
those people places and things before me who got murdered,
checking out my reflection in the rearview mirror.

Domesticity

i stopped into the stuffed and overcrowded morphine inn
of murder and mayhem, and the first people i saw when
entering were gertrude stein and alice b. toklas who very
benignly yet blankly with glazed-over eyes started glaring
at me, while strangely at the same time, had their backs
turned from me, and me being the very naturally rebellious
and sensitive chameleon that i had always been, and the fact
that they knew me, i pretended to sit in the other empty seats
which i could tell did not strike them as too funny, nor get my
dry and sleazy slapstick sense of humor. i told them in both french
and english that i was only kidding and proceeded to just get up,
as this vacation was to be spent in an ancient and abandoned
decadent section of Île de la Cité where i had decided to take
my wife and kid and could tell this was going to be one of those
queer dreams about how mankind just believes and thrives off
gossip and rumors, worst and most absurd traits and character-
istics of human nature (lacking in nuance, or for that matter
substance) as opposed to the integrity and sincerity of one's
character; there was a motorcyclist who of course being the
actor that he was decided to very 'dumb' just sit right behind
me, primping his beard and leather duds, pretending to look all
mean and scary, but us being from the boroughs never particularly
impressed or intimidated by this attention-seeking behavior,
and had them casually get up and take another booth and after i was
done writing a couple notes on a cocktail napkin followed them
through the tavern of insane tourists; the sort which i liked so
much more than the chorus of cookie-cutter ones who always
 seemed obsessed in trying to get your approval with their
rules and regulations of etiquette and culture and pathetically
begging for your validation. when i proceeded to head down
the aisle i could see a waitress start to become enamored by me and
flirt with me, but looked exactly like some recent half-crazed
girlfriend in a relationship which had just ended abruptly, and at
that moment, believe i could tell i was dreaming and plopped
myself right down next to my wife and kid

Rimbaud and verlaines getting old on benches
people-watching the gigantic and grotesque marionettes,
the dwarf from monmartre, slut-virgins having just escaped

the prisons of aristocratic castles of third cousins on the
outskirts of the suburbs, and that unsung poet also
a dope addict walking his infamous pet lobster

Pockets full of bullets, foreign currency
and shells from the sea which led
me to le gare de lyon and nice and
the border of italy where the train
workers are religiously on strike
on my way to the ferry and
a whole other form of
temporary 'sanity'
and freedom.

Vitamin C (and the case of the harassing fraud inspector)

1

these days
the wife, life,
even the kid
driving me crazy
all just trying to get
the last word in edgewise
and i'm just trying to get by
just trying to get things
straight and right and
decide as a last resort
to turn on the radio
and the good ol'
moody blues
come on
(they got this keen
phenomenon where
they always seem to
just be lingering around
out there somewhere
between the airwaves
and nature permeating
your tortured heart and
soul, a band you totally
forgot about, a band think
a lot of people forgot about)
where that lead singer
forgot his name going
out of his way to give
straight-up and sincere
advice and think bruce
was right–"we learned
more from a 3 minute
record than we ever
learned in school"
sometimes i think
all you can really

do is turn to the radio
leaves turning scarlet
and crimson-blaze
outside window

2

i like what rimbaud said when he said he remembers
when he was born and crawled across the bed
i like what nietzsche said when he said
he felt like he was born a very old man
i get it! i get it! i fucken get it!
feeling like getting the choice
(not really) of whether to
be stoned to death or a gun
to the head while offering your
wife to plant tulip bulbs with your
son in the back of the wilderness
i like how voltaire at the end of
"candide" just had him spending
the rest of his days in the garden
those awful complaining gossiping
old women in "old man goriot"
and "crime and punishment"

3

don't tell me when it starts to come down
like one of those snow globes doesn't
heal all things broken and fragile...

4

"i got the fraud inspector
breathing down my neck
cuz someone ripped off my shit
while trying to build back credit!"

5

"oo-wwh won't you tell me again...
oo-wwh can you feel it...?"

Make Hay While Rome's Burning

nowadays we watch
    the house & senate
               hearings
                    (nobody
                        listening
                to nobody
                all that sleazy scape-
                    goating & sucker-
                    punching & stoning)
                trying to keep up
                keep in good shape
                              up on our tread-
                                    mill
          get pizza & painkiller
                delivered
  & going through the motions
                  & routine & ritual
                          of becoming
        more "complete people"
    only certain killers
let in on the riddle.

5:35

watching over
my local cable
"daddy issues"
showing this
caption of
'young dad'
getting advice
from an 'old dad'
 (can't stand both
of them...) with a
nutter caption which
reads "igotdaddyissues
google.com" while across
the way in the community
garden find myself entranced
with this young vibrant spirited
girl full of mad heart bending over
with her shovel like some vagabond
angel gracefully stabbing at the ground
digging me a very quick convenient grave

they always seem to take
off slowly without me

only time i feel taken seriously...

For e.e. cummings

had been driving
down the strip-
mall at night
& suddenly
saw those
glowing
golden
arches
lit up
bright
in the
dying
distance
with that
in famous
mantra–
"billions
& billions
served"
& could
aint help
but think
this be
some thing
of our holy
journey
to mecca
once saw
this vividly
in my dreams
dreaming down
some long-
lost sacred
sparkling
ancient
boujeause
boulevard
in egypt
should

have
invested
in ibm
& disney
ages ago.

The Ancient Contemporary Pyramids:
Somewhere Right Around The Reservoir Or How To Do
Underage Drinking & Make Something In 3 Unequal Parts

I.

Looking back i really liked and so much hated
whenever that teacher would ask you to write
a paper about what you did the previous summer
as how could you really explain or translate making
models of battleships and airplanes with your burnout
buddies getting wasted all day sniffing model glue caddying
for these awful ungrateful wall streeters and their snobby sons
and daughter-in-laws killing yourself carrying golf bags over your
shoulder for 18 holes spending your pittance of tip money cruising
to the ghetto to do bronx-runs to pick up a couple dime bags
listening all day to the clash and the who and doors and bob marley
looking strong and sculpted and bronzed and handsome and trying
to get laid ending walking down the aisle of suburban streets in the
deep dark evening with your wise ass buddies in your *fruit of the loom*
underwear cracking riddles before we snuck into neighbor's back-
yards and howling like madmen doing cannonballs off diving
boards then being dropped off drunk to your front lawn i mean
how could you really explain or translate this to some stuffy
english teacher about what you did the previous summer as
just really felt like absolutely nothing but guess looking back
a hell of a lot did happen

II.

Marriage some
times a mirage
between prison
& not even
existing
would
it be
so much
a stretch

to be
self-
mood
lately
or pudding
bullet straight
in my brain
while kid's
chess tutor
tutoring him
on the ways
of the world
& defenses
& strategies
walking the
highwire
lowlife
liar
between
maddening
routines
& rituals
of moody
mess
domesticity
& wisps of
wild beautiful
vagabond girl
with hair
flowing
flaming
flirting
roaming
the streets
& seasons
& seeing
threw
every
thing
pin
cushion

clouds
start
coming
down
& head
to the pin
nickel of
mountain
in the heart
of nirvana
to discover
whole new
chinese
takeout
& deliberately
stray home
beneath
the stars
on an un
known
route
to try
& get
lost
& forget
myself
to find
myself
once
more

III.

When do the ghosts show up?
cuz sure as heck could use
the shut eye during
those deep dark
lonely parts
of the night

how did *the who* put it?
"i want to drown
in cold water..."

```
A Slice (with nothing i mean everything on it)
```

1

I'm nor sure if I'm experiencing some-
thing of a mid-life crisis but watching
the local news over my TV station

I dream of being chased across
the field by the girl's field hockey
team and getting flogged to death

2

The last they'll see of me will be
something of a pained smile like
that expression smelling the roses

3

Vermont vs. Niagara...

4

Your son wrestling
a tomboy on your front lawn
both blushing and giving it all they got

5

Your wife very focused and intense
cuts out coupons for the upcoming holiday

6

Has America become all comfortably
choreographed and aerobic with white
housewives from the suburbs throwing punches
and quick karate kicks (to get rid of excess flab)
turning to black gangsters from the ghetto?

7

ibid: I don't know? If the FBI can put Dillinger
as their poster boy target for America's most wanted
why can't they do the same for Trump and that chump Bannon?
Whenever I think of them instantly get nauseous and the Hershey squirts

8

("So you don't say..."
so says Curly

9

Or was that Ludwig
Wittgenstein?

10

Ludwig Van...
Clockwork Orange)

11

We put a man on the moon
boots on the ground
and all we got

to show for it
is global warming
and a girl who can't

even get off her
cell phone while
crossing the road

12

Kerouac bends over to tie his sneaker
at the change of seasons in the middle
of the muddy ball field and watches
the sun go down over the mountain
as all turns silent and silhouetted

beatific and blessed...

13

Methadone is to heroin
as sex is to existence

14

Pillow talk is the re-
mains of all resistance.

A Tourist Guide To Nodding-Out

1. some
     where
         be-
             tween
human nature
& bullshit
& pathologies
   (lies...)
         amerika
    (& time to)
              fill up
                   yaw
     rickshaw, piñata
                with junk mail
       & drop it back down
                        river
              like baby moses
                   praying for a miracle
                        (time to follow your dreams...
                        screams of the ice cream man)

2.   gotta get back to haifa
                    mafia ferry
                 for naples/sicilia
                    where the old
                          southern pizans
           shaved my tired
                    wandering
                        vagabond skull
                              with a straight-edge
                                   (like spatulas
                          wielded wildly
                  by japanese magicians
           during spoiled princesses
sweet-sixteens
    who would all
        eventually marry
             rabbis or pediatricians)

   offering me shots
       of espresso
           & desperately-needed
                conversation

   although i didn't understand it
       but the ambiance & atmosphere
            meant the world
 & healed a broken & shattered heart
     from those nonchalant schmucks
          oblivious & fluent
             at not getting it

3. back to the catskills, y'israel
   sprawling holy hills & discos
     forgot what it felt like
        the pretty young
           poverty-stricken
            decadent
              jewish girls

4.   those ancient sacred plain trees
& winding cobblestone streets of nice which
seemed to hold one's fate & destiny dingle
peninsula bed & breakfasts of lonely mad
women & widows at the end of the world
& beautiful blushing daughters in aprons
minding their business serving me my
tea & paper & simply returning it to the
creaking miniature lopsided hall outside
the keyhole where your only mantra be
the wail of a wild whispering windy sea

5.   would have loved to have heard
       buddy holly's–
        "everyday it's a' getting closer..."
          translated into flamenco

6. holiday season right around the corner
starting premature in the land of america
right around halloween & guess gotta

get ready for drinking & refrigerator
full of puerto rican rum & leftovers
& lamenting & triggers & memories

7. time to cut down the stalks of sunflowers
       & look out for wild turkey stealing down the mountain.

How To Not Lose It All (and regain perspective and be reborn) In The Bathroom Of A Sunoco

Loneliness finally got hemingway and kerouac
in the end while they were getting ready and
dressed in the giant grandfather clock before
they accepted their awards. jean-paul sartre
based purely on principle refused to accept
his nobel prize and courageously rebelliously
told them so in his speech to the committee.
after everything he did for them they threw
chaplin out of the country. did something
similarly to lenny bruce and john lennon.
my wife wrecked my favorite decorative
pillow with the zebra on it taking it off
the sofa to watch her dramas and now
cotton comes out of the bottom. i hate
the times we live in and now a number of
basketball stars will refuse to play for their
coach (or actually start their own team up)
and all of sudden the front office will fire
them and never a thank you or seen from
or heard from again as if they don't have
to put bread on the table of their families.
the hypnotic rattling sound of the lumber
trucks carrying their loads of long sappy
logs rumbling over bridges in the distance
and not too distant future keeps my head
in the game and settled and sane and even
helps make sense of my nightmares keeping
my life based in reality like that excruciating
unavoidable loneliness which inevitably
struck kerouac and hemingway getting
ready in their great grandfather clocks
when the mist came down from the
mountain and the factory and
ferries at the break of day.
here come the foghorns
and lay of the land
and stray light like
eggs over easy...

```
The Weather
```

i decided in my next
                life
  gonna just be
         one of those
                  medicine
           cabinets
   & live all snug
like a bug
in a rug
    inside
         one of those
              mad scientist
                   metallic shelves
         all full of ointments
& elixirs & pain killers
& make a killing
     living happily ever after
          keeping it cracked open just slightly
                  to get a feel of the seasons
                     & let in the dusk & dawn
                                     every so often
                         all those artificial
                         natural scents
                         of what's that?
                              spearmint?
                                  peppermint?
                                  eucalyptus?
                                     to get you
out of your indifference
            still can't get that song out of my head...

Sears Roebuck

In the morning i call up *sears* repair and i swear they say
something like–"i am a real-life computer and you can ask
me any question, try me…" and i'm thinking you gotta be
fucken kidding, as already reached that boiling point i've
reached so many times previously growing up in the bullshit
and bureaucracy of the big city, and can't help but to be slightly
sarcastic and desperate and ask it specific questions about
marriage…about global warming and the apocalypse…about
dreams and nightmares…how and if they can heal a broken and
damaged heart and soul…what they do about all that plaque build-
up and gunk from all those jealous little devils and posers in the
world who come a dime a dozen and just get so bored…last but
not least, the repeated patterns of the publishing business who put
you under contract and then never return your e-mails or calls and
fall off the end of the world…finally, and no shock at all, get a long
vacant space of silence of mock hesitation and then even more
torture, asking me to constantly repeat my question, while with
this contrived, feigned, human-like interest says–"i didn't get that"
(real shocker like some girl who once loved you having turned
indifferent) and like a modern day ralph kramden with tourette's,
retort in monotone–"go fuck yourself" and keep on pressing zero
over and over again until i get one of those real-life humans
who appear to be reading straight off some choreographed tele-
marketer script and ask her if i can somehow get that computer again.

Wake-Up Call

Life often presents as the same old card trick
where you open up your cupboard and the exact
same suffering and sorrow (and just learn to accept
and deal with it, while in the stack, serendipitously,
come upon the exact same plate with that snowman
with his arms wide open) maybe just the symptoms
and patterns of Buddhism with all that pain and
suffering thinking back in the back of your mind
sure was a fine trip out to the sputtering lamplight.

Department Zero

you know i guess i get missing
knives forks spoons whole cutlery
sets, cups and glasses (honestly
lying really don't get it at all)
all your socks and shit like that
past girlfriends best friends
strangers and acquaintances
who in my opinion were really
the best and most reliable of all
but how in the heck good ol' silk
beautiful brown suits which used
to hang in your closet like a past
partner at the end of the tracks in
coney island; wonderful wrinkled
linen suits i picked up on the cheap
on le promenade des anglais when used
to wander europe all by my lonesome
and probably at my most contented
(looking back, calm, cool and collected
whatever the fuck that looked like) suits
i used to nod out in when taking the ferry
from the lower east side to new jersey, now
leaving me simply with a big empty vacant
closet hole in my soul down on my luck full
of memories and moments, so i guess i get
losing all that shit, but deep down inside
when i really think about it not exactly.

Pain Killer

my wife is very organized. i looked up at her calendar
stuck to our refrigerator and next monday said "kill husb
with shov." of course this piqued my interest a little and
decided to proceed to the following week, and wasn't too
surprised to see "fune" and 'don't forget to bring the potato
salad and salmon and couscous cilantro, and basil from the
garden;' don't know if this is impulsive and if she's gonna get
angry, but thought what else do i really have to lose? scribbled in
dill as feel everything goes well with dill, then signed my initials.

Right Before They Walked On The Moon

i always like to watch young couples at ballgames
as always seem so full of hope and spirit and
innocence and that life hasn't gotten to them.
my parents first met when my father was
a dentist and my mother was his patient.
he was thirty and she was sixteen and
they got instantly married and moved
to this new housing complex called
le havre which looked over some
harbor in whitestone, queens
and my mother told me she
saw the whole whitestone
bridge being pieced together
from their top-floor apartment
but had to move from the neighbor-
hood 'cause my dad kept on bumping
into his patients and couldn't remember
their names; always seemed like an
awfully strange reason to leave, but
who am i to say and ended up having
three kids and moving to new rochelle
the fictional home of dick van dyke
and mary tyler moore when he had
that great big *dentyne* smile and used
to very nimble and agile with slapstick
style dodge or leap over that piece
of furniture in their sunken black
and white, sepia living room in
the opening credits, where everything
still seemed so open to the imagination
or some grand inside joke of existence
and they ended up moving to this dead
end at the blissful end of the world with
plush lawns so plush could still dig holes
all the way to china or burn leaves with
magnifying glasses and no one would
get into trouble, as it felt like neighbors
still cared and gave a damn about each
other and were kind and thoughtful and

kids would grow like laundry on the line,
avocados on the sill, shortcuts through
the woods, and perverts on the roof.

you lived off a.m. radio
which was your truth
and was your moon.

denouement: ironically now find myself
watching the ball game late at night
choking to death on sulfites reflecting
how i don't deserve my wife, the saint
that she is, the saint that i'm not
and turn to those young couples
cracking-up in the crowd over
their feast of beer and hotdogs
exactly the way we were, and
of course the mets falling behind
the yankees in *the subway series*
6-3, guess the way things are just
deemed to be and suppose that
old cliche really does ring true;
as long as you got your memories
which always grounds me and helps
to keep things in perspective and turn
over a new leaf and fall fast asleep…

how to wake up from the dream
and keep your wits about you.

Coping & Survival Skills

i was thinking this real dreary overcast autumn day
seeing all the leaves blowing past my windowpane
from one season to the next, wouldn't it be brilliant
to have like one of those handy tanks of nitrous-oxide
just hanging around; have one of those homebound hygienists
just hanging around always with a kind smile and nice thing to
say maybe even give her a free room and board in the basement
(where she can feel free to wear those white hospital sneakers,
romance novels and the bible, croon tom jones and mac davis)
having absolutely nothing to do with that cult thriller "blue velvet"
and whenever i need her just press that private button near my
easy chair and shows up with that kind smile and nice thing
to say and mask and tank and applies it to my face; keeps
me to a strict and rigid regiment, as-needed, twice a day
for a bit of escape; always felt a part of things and free
when got out the chair and got back on the crosstown
to the # 7 in flushing; little more liberated little
less alienated back to my railroad on rivington.

Third Cousin To Caligula

i want to go back
to old girlfriends
who desire
to kill me
or do me
in be one of
those psychotic
constellations
where they
make connections
from star to star
like some sort of
foreboding figure
lurking with an
ice pick and rag mop
to know the real true
mysteries of existence
lie somewhere between
fate and coincidence...

After Confession

i would want i just go
to one of those reunions
of ol' tomboys and thugs
from the neighborhood
and the ones who start
brawling are the drunken
tomboys in the leaves
of front lawns and pick
themselves up and finally
a slow dance between
the tomboys and thugs
(always when it comes
down the most modest
and humble) nursing
each other back
to health.

we all return home
below streetlamps
with a deeper
sense of self.

Boogie Wonderland (what it means to be a man)

i remember when rod stewart's song came out
'if you want my body and you think i'm sexy'
and was age 13 where in the jewish
religion you were deemed to be a man
and all felt like a sham or i felt like a sham
with my white boy afro and three piece suit
and tie with soccer players on it disco dancing
at some roller rink or banquet hall surviving off
pigs in blankets and those tiny egg rolls and i
guess yes had a pretty good body and was pretty
sexy (really not sure and hard to tell) and just a
year later they showed all those disco albums
getting blown to pieces in what stadium think
it may have been shea or somewhere in detroit
or chicago as if sacrificing a virgin with the slogan
"disco sucks" and thought how dare they do this
and what does this represent as in my subconscious
think had felt i had worked too long and hard at it to
become a man whatever the hell that meant and what's
with all this manufactured anger and what was to come
later, as honestly, ironically, the next decade and
generation was the one that sucked the big one.

Dusk Radio

if i could
i would
buy u
a life
time
supply
of sushi
on a weekly
basis matter
of fact i'd
have the sushi
guy come over
with his kind wife
in her kimino and
personally roll it
on our kitchen island
i'd give you all those
vacations i owe you
i couldn't afford all
those places we
never got to in
italy and spain
what'ya say?
antigua and
that antebellum
island right off
the coast of
the carolinas
right off
the coast
of texas
got a
mustang
in it
not too
far from
your friend
from the bronx
who used to die

her hair in kool
aid packets
matter of
fact give
you a
summer
home in
the good
part of
the boogie
down and
winterhome
in brighton
beach not
too far
above those
old russian
yentas who
gather on
benches
in their
furcoats
and look
out to the
atlantic
they got
an opiate
problem
out here
and won't
even give
you pain
killer as
needed
yeah i'd
give you
all those
things
needed
vegas
before

it be
came
vegas.

The First Snow On The Mountain On Top Of Hospital Hill

i went
back & forth
with my client
with asperger's today
about if they dropped
a hydrogen bomb on
nagasaki. i said they
did not and they were
both atomic (as if any
of that would matter)
and they were still
fidgeting around
with it like the
double-helix
or some really
cute slow country
girl futile forlorn
trying to calculate
your expenses for
your cheeseburger
and fries alongside
the side of the road
at one of those road
side stands while
the line grows longer
and longer. any which
way we talked about
more and accomplished
far more in the course
of our rapport than any
one of those marines
they like to so often talk
about who do more before
the whole world wakes up
or one of those really
pompous managers
at *walmart* with his
grandiose episodes
thinking he knows

it all and never left
the borders of his folk
lore. tornadoes have
struck a month earlier
in the northern plains.

```
Falling In Love With That Fine Country
Girl With A Good Head On Her Shoulders
As Humble As Pie Right By The Meat Aisle
```

You wait for your client in the parking lot
looking for the perfect junk food and start
to listen to good ol' Billy Joel singing that
piano lounge love song–"I love you just
the way you are" which in its simplicity
you know is so profound something
about 'I don't need nothing clever
just someone to talk to' and think
back to those ancient Egyptians
and wonder if they had the same
inclinations and issues laid back in
lean-to's just outside the silhouetted
pyramids; the tire and log trucks go
rambling by from Vermont to Canada
and back and forth across the border
and there are angels serving you your
coffee at *Dunkin Donuts* and know all
it ever comes down to are these wishes
and dreams and fragments and forms
which is all a part of the folklore
lost somewhere between
fantasy and everything
you ever hoped for.

Early Noon After The Deluge

The woman in the booth next to me at the library
starts to just naturally breakdown weeping, tears
streaming down her cheeks, and instinctively
I think might really be able to help her, but
have been through the same kind of crises
and know deep down inside, not a heck
of a lot I can do; that it's just one of those
things, unfortunately, with time, she's going
to have to get through. After this, she starts
to do some really deep, heavy, rhythmic
breathing, almost as if naturally engaged
in pure ecstasy, of which I am totally sym-
pathetic and in sync (I think of all those summer
romances on the lake). Older women, silently, very
politely vanish with their shrink-wrapped books, while
finally turned to spring through the glazed windows
of the library in this beat down, depressed town
of Vermont; angels run up and down the steps
of the opera house, boys who go un noticed,
camouflaged by the trees and boxcars and
haunted houses of backyards, patiently explore
the perimeter of the town along the traintracks
while the postman with his big stuffed sack
precisely, letter by letter, moves from home
to home; the gravediggers on their lunch
break, take on the role of absolutely
no place to escape, nowhere to go
just like everyone else, just like
these storms, which seem to
redeem and clean it all up
and make it all glow.

Right Around The New England Doll Factory

As it's that part of the season
where you're so goddamn
exhausted & drained
& you're just trying
to make your way
& all just one
big hustle
(& bustle)
& the snow
drifts are so
dirty & filthy
& the muddy
ice cream trucks
still making their
daily deliveries
& large ladies
leaving pubs
with great big
smiles as though
just got into a tussle
taking out bartenders
& the young boys
from the neighborhood
are being escorted in hand-
cuffs by their wrists & ankles
to their fate & day in court
& the high school angels
heading home in pickups
pouting & sulking
& to die for
with demure
smiles & see
exactly what
they'd throw
it all away for
that very tall
svelte one
who looks
like a cross

between
a basketball
star & thug
always
seeming
to be doing
something illegal
& on the downlow
somewhere between
the merchant stores
& river & boxcars
which stop by
every so often
& the old ladies
at the library
rapping about
deadly diseases
& just trying
to make it
on a day
by day
basis
& you're just
trying to make it
home for your rum & coke
& dose of flowers & chocolate
for your girl you feel awful got into
an absurd petty war the night before

Smoke still flows right around
the new england doll factory...

```
I Think My Wife Would Be Far Happier If
I Was A Big Bottle Of Blue Cleaning Fluid
```

and could
just ditch me
and carry me
all around
the home
up and
down
the stairs
obviously
in the bath
room and
kitchen
when she
had our
friends
over
all those very
fancy-schmanzy
mature dinner
dates adults
go on when
they're all
grown up
with their
friends who
are accountants
insurance men
and dentists
in the passenger
seat riding shotgun
to her 9-5 job being
a substitute teacher
in her queen-sized bed
falling asleep to *law & order*
going on vacation to club med
or those all-inclusive cruises
to family get-togethers
and funerals and reunions

to spas and to visit her ma
think my wife would be
far happier if i was a
big bottle of blue
cleaning fluid.

Making The Scene

I've decided gonna just be
one of those centerpieces
of wax fruit placed smack
dab in the middle of one
of those awful horrible
dining room tables
as believe upon
retrospect always
had a slight bit
of a social phobia
nor ever really had a heck
of a lot to say to the guests
as always liked them so much
better from that perspective
and think would just feel far
more comfortable just sitting
there as an undercover bowl
of wax fruit next to some
unused dusty piano and
whole half-crazed family
with insane pasted-on
smiles looking down
on me from some
family gathering
from some picture
frame just hanging
there suspended
in time with
my ear bent
to that good
ol' grandfather
clock going off
on the hour
lulled
to sleep
lulled
by trauma
and triggers
and rigid reminders

of 3, 4, 5, 6 in the morning
ya gotta be kidding! reason
wanna be a centerpiece
of one of those bowls
of wax fruit just being
left the hell alone if you
kinda get where i'm going?
like that cruise ship made up
of string stuck in a bottle
till the end of time
sailing off to eternity.

Vinnie Barbarino

Last night in trying to get to bed
i came upon an old rerun of
welcome back kotter where
it was sadie-hawkins day
where the girls ask out
the guys and vinnie
barbarino played
by that young sly
pick-up artist
john travolta
still didn't
have a date
and mr. kotter
played by gabe
kaplan one of
the worst actors
and non-funny guys
of all time tried to explain
in one of those long awful
drawn-out dialogues that
it all had to do with his
attitude and pride and
started to reflect and
think back to my life
in how much wasted
time gone by acting
like vinnie barbarino
while getting lost
with the wife
trying to find
that chinese
buffet
somewhere
in one of those
beautiful
broken
down
towns
strung-out

right around
the remnants
and rubble
of one of
those radiant
ramshackle
mountains

Probably explains
why i can't stand
getting lost most
of the time...

Something Like Redemption

i can't begin to tell you why the christmas tree lights
shine so bright and have come together so nice this
time this time of year like an orchestra like a jigsaw
puzzle like animal crackers like the blinking burning
stars balanced way up above over our barn in the
middle of the deep dark night i can't begin to tell
you why the old time movies muted on my tv just
seem to keep me such better company and don't
finally at last leap off my screen i can't begin to tell
you why when i down those heartbreak pills really
heartburn meds gotten by my wife washed down
with a shot of seltzer straight out the refrigerator
tonight it all seems to just go down so much better
and cure and heal all my nightmares and insomnia
i can't begin to tell you why "memphis vs. new orleans"
looks so fine and why that guy they affectionately call
monobrow on new orleans who is their only good player
while just stands there all by his lonesome right in the
middle of my living room at courtside with those long
arms dangling by his side and a slight sardonic smile
looking as if he's seen it all just looks like a really nice
and humble guy i can't begin to tell you why it all just
somehow seems right me standing here naked in my
kitchen at 3:30 in the morning just like monobrow after
all those long miserable down in the dump years i spent
suffering down there in new orleans not knowing a single
solitary soul me solitary and on my own without a friend
to call my own i can't begin to tell you why at this exact
moment naked not wanted dead or alive standing in my
kitchen at 3:30 in the morning with the christmas tree
glistening monobrow beaming everything seems right.

The Secret To The Secret Of Buried Treasure

The other morning I just walked into the kitchen
and my little kid was just sitting at the island
with a gigantic bowl of *Rice Krispies* in milk.
He likes to go through the whole ritual of
burying all the Rice Krispies with his spoon
before he eats them until he's sure they're
all good and buried and the fine texture
and consistency of grout. I asked Dylan–
"What are you doing?" He said–"I'm looking
for the prize." I responded–"I don't think it's in there."
he said–"Yes it is…" I challenged him–"I don't think
so" and with the perseverance only a child is capable
of, and after going at it for at least five minutes or so
what'ya know, how it usually ends up working out
in the long-run, he proved me wrong and said–
"Daddy, here it is" and in one final fell swoop
scooped up the miniature skull of Han Solo.

After A Rough Night Of Dreaming

downpour coming
down in mountain

trail of cowboy music left on
on kid's radio in the morning.

Cult:or

Today when I asked Dylan how did it go with his trip to the museum he said that they wouldn't let you touch anything and everything was off-limits (I thought that sounds about right) and had great big spaces where they kept all the creepy dolls. He said when he took the bus home he just wanted to sit alone and stared out the window (which I wholeheartedly condoned).

Insomnia   -for g. stein one more time

these days i'm not sleeping so much. matter of fact
there are no facts. to the matter. no matters. and not
much at all. and can only can with the rays of the tv
on. with the weather on. with the sweet sound of the weather
girl's voice on. with the weather girl on me. with the figure
of the weather girl's figure on me. could die happily ever
after in my sleep. no funerals. no ceremonies. no one
knowing with the weather going. always seems to be
starting and to be stirring somewhere around sioux falls.
moving east to the dakotas. to montana. where as a child
i learned all about those domestic foreign exotic rivers
and tributaries and brave and courageous indian tribes.
who were they? sioux? iroquois? some low. some high
pressure coming down from canada. down around
great lakes. whatever those are again? michigan?
superior? huron? think i got them all. eery? eerily
sliding. sidling and sneaking right before sunrise
from the midwest right into the fine state of new york.
those parts i never heard of or been to. mostly think
where they keep all those institutions and prisons.
moving over the adirondacks and onto lake champlain.
and showing up to where i am right now. up in the north
country. not too far from vermont. new hampshire. maine.
where they got all those insanely pretty girls who are
french tutors and teach guitar lessons. live poverty-
stricken with missing parents looking down from
their pink haunted ramshackle victorians onto the
flooding river and village and the hitchers. who i
get more from than i ever did from anything in culture.
and decide to finally leave the thankless social work
business and get back into hospitality where i go on
all these interviews and think i'm really impressing
them (not trying to impress them yet know just from
life and experience am far more impressive than them)
and can talk circles around them. and don't ever
seem to return messages. even when i tell them
am totally flexible and available for practically
any shift. and try figuring out disconnects.
like do they even check out my references.

did my references check me out? and feels
like junior high school all over again which
by no coincidence was a total nightmare.
which i have absolutely no desire to revisit.
so just go fuck it. and can only fall back
to sleep again when i dream of those two
country sisters i met from the forest which
i developed a fine rapport and relationship
on one of my long jaunts and journeys
and rapped with by the rising river
under the snowy bridge babbling
down the mountain. and can only
imagine a ménage-a-trois but not
sexual or erotic kind but the kind
which just seems totally benign
and intimate and intellectual and
affectionate. and finish it off with
real pillow talk in the wilderness
by the babbling brook babbling
down the mountain under the
snowy bridge. literally roll out
of bed like some sort of animated
personified weather vane. and spread
myself out. muted. muffled. silhouetted.
against the venetian blinds. like jesus
crucified. mime cock-a-doodle doo
into the putrid silence of suburbs.

Ambiance

Out here in Vermont they got a lot
of great shit like chickens and roosters
and cows and goats, even the new trend
raising alpacas; well me thinking being
something of a New York kid am gonna
just start raising pigeons. I don't give a
flying what the tourists or neighbors think
and maybe get them shipped-in from Herald
Square around *Macy's* when the sun goes down
at dusk where all the bums and madmen and single
women hang out; figure be pretty economical as well
and can just feed them like pieces of hotdog bun or hot
pretzel or knishes and won't be like one of those crunchy
wannabe liberals but be like good ole Mike Tyson or Brando
on the rooftop, even Burt Lancaster trying to once again turn over
a new leaf in his prison cell in 'Birdman of Alcatraz.' You know
who I think would have made a really damn fine dynamic duo
for Vice President and Prez? Zero Mostel and Buddy Hackett.

```
A Mild Case Of Disassociative Fugue
```

In going today for a hospitality business interview
i asked at the front desk if there was a lisa or jennifer
i could talk to. they said they do have a lisa and a kim
but not a jennifer and suddenly i remembered those were
my babysitters way back when from when i was a kid. i've
been doing a lot of this recently and realize things truly do come
around full circle and maybe even a slight bit obtuse and diagonal.

A Botched Life

Man i'd take a job a second job even third
at *cumberland* to try and convince you
to provide you to rid me of all these
absurd emotions and feelings of guilt
shoot myself in the head like some
classic literal armed robbery
and absolutely no one would
know exactly how i want to go
and right before i do it stick
all the bills from the register
into a nice clean envelope
and send it out to you straight
up to your glistening lit window
in that blissful ramshackle haunted
victorian up on top the hill above the diner

Special on kleenex and gyros…

Putting Together A Badminton Set With A Passive-Aggressive Divorcee Talking About Lobotomies And Electric Shock Therapy On Memorial Day

Today the wife and I tried to put up one of those badminton nets they make it impossible to connect with all of those cheap plastic parts with one of my son's friends moms, an impossible woman as everyone's divorced out here and they're all hostile and passive-aggressive towards men, and constantly have to prove you're not one of them or representative of every man who ever walked out on them or did them in or betrayed them, and suppose since you're a clinical therapist, always feel obligated to take you hostage about diagnoses and medication, and laymen-like, how all of a sudden become authorities on the subject, how they're so vehemently against it from their couple of bad experiences (with DSS and husbands and best friends and you get it) and all so damn green and crunchy out here knowing absolutely nothing about the influence and effect of profound or severe pathologies or diagnoses, or chemical disequilibrium or maladaptive thinking, while with these impossible and futile exchanges, they ironically seem something like the perfect candidate, and always so damn aloof and arrogant, somehow becoming experts not realizing I'm not necessarily always so much a supporter of it or advocate, but one of these types of know-it-all women, who ask you questions and when you start answering start conveniently ignoring, making absolutely no eye contact, distant and determined with conviction and don't listen to a word you're saying, and just go on with their all-knowing goombya opinions and agenda and then somehow out of nowhere get on the subject of lobotomies and electric shock therapy, while your wife is reading the directions (of how to put together a badminton set) and find yourself getting more and more frustrated, trying to put together this object of leisure you thought was going to be simple instant-gratification, and forced to have to explain in gross detail the history of the shock factories of the 1950's, while even later on in certain institutionalized mileau environments; the patients of which you have known a couple and worked with, often were given ultimatums or none at all, rarely of their own will and volition, and of course with all this counter-transference and displacement and overcompensation battle of the sexes or quasi-liberalism try to engage you in their futile game of opposites not listening to a single word you're saying, and I'm thinking (with some of the other shit she's saying) you Munchausen madwoman, why the fuck are you even asking or for that matter on our property? Didn't even want to meet you in the first place, which ironically, feels very much against my own will and volition and something of an ultimatum, 'cause said she wanted to meet me and here I am debating with some freak under the blazing sun, being tormented by some miserable single woman, who hates men talking about lobotomies and electric shock therapy, trying to put together a freaken badminton set (just to watch those free-sailing birdies and get my slight taste of freedom) whose plastic parts are scattered all over the lawn. luckily she took off to pick up a couple watermelons for some dysfunctional family get-together, and finally at last, after feeling wasted and wired, took my first breath in don't know how long…

Creature-Feature

i decided if
i ever become
filthy rich i'm
gonna buy me
one of those
drive-ins and
be a concessionist
holed-up in
a ticket booth
watching all of
half-crazed culture
pass right in front
of my eyes,
the young
lovers,
divorcees,
gangbangers,
freaks and
grotesques
those on
suicide watch
of do or die
dysfunctional
existence while
i grow old
and retire
right there
on the spot
all safe & secure
in that tiny little box
nodding out to my
joyce & proust
while i simply see
the light from the
projectionist show
up on the horizon
just outside the land
of providence rhode
island and know

finally after a life
time of suffering
i'm a free man
the most sane
sort of asylum.

```
Ho-Jo's
```

I have decided when family life is getting to me
when wife is being a nudge and driving me crazy
i'm gonna build my own private *howard johnson*
underground one of those with the long bleak
midnight ice cream counters where no one
ever goes where that faceless miserable
waitress in her uniform the same color
of the empty booths and stools and
of course great big empty bathrooms
which always brings me back to earth
and grounds me and only leave when
i'm good and ready and head out those
silvery swinging doors out to the big bleak
empty midnight highway a new man taking
in the great empty melancholy swathes of
leftover scents of rain and breeze and being
and beautiful spirits of broken ghost histories

To know the true-blue core of silence
lies in the blessed solitude of seasons
whispering all those sweet nothings
to girls you loved and believe
it or not loved me as well.

Before The Invention Of Paradise

Give me an island
right off the caribbean
yet to be discovered
a paper delivered
with nothing in it
your forecast
from bismark,
minneapolis, denver,
the great pyramids
gorgeous women
roaming around
the souvenir shops
without their masters
with everything already ripped-
off due to their acting-out and
impulse disorders (no winking
glossy magazines, no disco ball,
no limbo lower now) cliff divers
and steel drummers and gigolos
having no place else to roam,
chameleons, jesus christ lizards,
rastas scaling the bent boughs
of palm trees to try and impress
pretty white daughters from
the suburbs into the silent
bleak paradise of eternity
half-crazed vampires
sneaking quick peeks
through sleazy curtains
of peeping-tom bedrooms
vultures keeping their
distance from the greedy
tourists, silhouetted way up
on top of palms, modest and
introspective in the morning
an origami sun and
an origami seashore

You creep back into your conch shell where all you hear is the self-soothing murmur of–"more, more, more, how do you like it? how do you like it?"

"Were you being ironic?"

On The Origins Of Drinking & Dart Playing

Recently to allay some of my anxiety and ruminating
I been watching a lot of those 1950's black & white
movies where 'the leisure class' living a life of leisure
always decked-out in really fine linen and flannel suits
and wives in those gigantic flowing flowerprint dresses
who hide inside all their safety and security and seduction
while I keep them all muted I try to somehow imagine
what's really happening and going on between them
and always seem to make great use of their homes
and gardens and parlors and vestibules and foyers
and lovely living rooms with bookcases and pianos
and sweeping staircases and got these specially
built-in bars in the basement with a lot of bamboo
and Naugahyde an extension of their identity and pride
and even their token dart boards I suppose with those
really sharp lethal points so can get in the real-life
and subconscious fantasy nightmare challenge
and element of danger of everyday existence
when all drunk and disoriented to keep up
with the lying and lascivious do or die rumors
of the very gregarious and intoxicating Jones'
I guess why way back when always seemed
to have a late-afternoon martini after-dinner
brandy available and in hand to try and
keep their head and wits about them

McCarthey hearings
in black & white static
muted on the TV stand.

The Rest Of That Song Heart & Soul

1

In all those
old black
& white films
full of preppies
in their beanies
caroling to
the heavens
i was the buffoon
behind the garden
wall laughing hysterically
mumbling under my breath
with my slice of pizza with
everything on it and a brown
paper bag full of shit ready to
light it on fire right on the doorstep
of the aristocrat's daughter i sincerely
loved as didn't know how to express
myself nor offer my hard(end) soul

2

I think later on at my funeral
i want to hire myself to play
the harmonica without that
whole schmaltzy band
behind me and those
cute jewish cousins
in their sky-blue
evening gowns
and sky-blue
mascara
with their
white-leather
pumps from
the island

who no
one knew who
they belonged
to and later
got turned
on to heroin
only showing
up to weddings
and bar-mitzvahs

3

I'll be the one
stealing glances
at you across
the room
blowing
spitballs
at you
don't pay
me no mind
for a good time...

4

Finally going off
on a long yodeling
jimmy rogers solo
as if finally
figuring
out the rest
of the lyrics
to the song
or even for
that matter
sum of
heart
& soul.

Internal Organ: how the end not too far from the very beginning

Even back then
they'd have
the skeleton
shadows splashed
out against the wall
which would draw
you right in to all
those real life true
blue conflicts & drama
of black & white b film-noirs
as complicated & conflicted
& lost & hollow as yours
& might even dissolve
& solve all your problems
As they'd splash
the rippling
shadows
of blinds
or even
the garden
into the parlor
which formed
a life of its own
like a flickering
candle & seep
& penetrate
all your senses
most importantly
your mind heart & soul
you thinking being so cool
the last scent of yourself
on your deathbed being
blown-out paraffin then
vanishing to the wind
in the multi-colored
misty change
of seasons.

Just Like One Of Those Streams Of Light
Which Comes Out Of The Projectionist
Booth On Some Dim Overcast Day

Through a sliver of the wilderness
you suddenly come upon the majestic
and miraculous pacific beat and bleary-
eyed almost unable to believe it which
is like some holy hallelujah hosanna
end of suffering start of it before
any of this ever began surviving
all the madmen having to be-
come madder with mad spirit
perseverance, and passion

A sleepwalker waking up
somewhere between life-
transition and the illusion.

```
The Female Clown With Man Problems & Mean Pastor
With An Attitude Taking The Hospital Elevator Up To
The Solarium Soulless Going Through The Motions
Forgetting What Their True Job & Purpose Is
```

I imagine death will be alot like
the scent of rubbing alcohol
without the smell just sitting
in some petri dish in some
mad scientist laboratory
waiting to be judged

Heaven will be the possibility
of a tuna melt and a leftover
slice of boston cream pie
you forgot in the fridge

Hell will be just the way i'm feeling
wasted, drained, beaten, betrayed
constantly feeding the toll over and
over again and ending up nowhere

You roll bleary-eyed out of bed...

Rawlings

So on his deathbed i guess makes
something of a final request and for
them to pick up one of those brand
new leather baseball mitts with a
rawling's baseball put inside it and
piece of twine wrapped tightly around
it as never was able to break it in
and make the perfect pocket and
whether this is some kind of fantasy
literally in an arrested stage of develop-
ment or not none of that really matters
and will live happily ever after with that
brand new baseball mitt and rawlings
baseball and a piece of twine rapped
around to keep it all in place placed
in between the mattress before he goes
to a better place and dies a happy man.

Acknowledgments

"Postcards From The Northern Plains" — *Ascent Aspiration*s

"Nanook" — *The Labletter - A Lonely Riot Magazine*

"Mock Apple Pie" and "A Different Sort Of Manifesto (manifest destiny)"
— *Thought Notebook Magazine*

"Saints & Hoboes" — *Joey and the Black Boots*

"Walmart" — *Parody*

"Just Off Walden", "The Lack Of Influence Of Media On The Lacking Individual", "Guest Villain" and "That Pretty Girl From Illinois"
— *Boston Poetry Magazine*

"Traveling" — *The Hungry Chimera*

"News From North Country" and "The Revolutionary War"
— *Projected Letters*

About Fomite

A fomite is a medium capable of transmitting infectious organisms from one individual to another.

"The activity of art is based on the capacity of people to be infected by the feelings of others." Tolstoy, *What Is Art?*

Writing a review on Amazon, Good Reads, Shelfari, Library Thing or other social media sites for readers will help the progress of independent publishing. To submit a review, go to the book page on any of the sites and follow the links for reviews. Books from independent presses rely on reader-to-reader communications.

For more information or to order any of our books, visit http://www.fomitepress.com/FOMITE/Our_Books.html

More Titles from Fomite...

Novels

Joshua Amses — *Ghatsr*
Joshua Amses — *During This, Our Nadir*
Joshua Amses — *Raven or Crow*
Joshua Amses — *The Moment Before an Injury*
Jaysinh Birjepatel — *The Good Muslim of Jackson Heights*
Jaysinh Birjepatel — *Nothing Beside Remains*
David Brizer — *Victor Rand*
Paula Closson Buck — *Summer on the Cold War Planet*
Dan Chodorkoff — *Loisaida*
David Adams Cleveland — *Time's Betrayal*
Jaimee Wriston Colbert — *Vanishing Acts*
Roger Coleman — *Skywreck Afternoons*
Marc Estrin — *Hyde*
Marc Estrin — *Kafka's Roach*
Marc Estrin — *Speckled Vanities*
Zdravka Evtimova — *In the Town of Joy and Peace*
Zdravka Evtimova — *Sinfonia Bulgarica*
Daniel Forbes — *Derail This Train Wreck*
Greg Guma — *Dons of Time*
Richard Hawley — *The Three Lives of Jonathan Force*
Lamar Herrin — *Father Figure*
Michael Horner — *Damage Control*
Ron Jacobs — *All the Sinners Saints*
Ron Jacobs — *Short Order Frame Up*

Ron Jacobs — *The Co-conspirator's Tale*
Scott Archer Jones — *And Throw the Skins Away*
Scott Archer Jones — *A Rising Tide of People Swept Away*
Julie Justicz — *A Boy Called Home*
Maggie Kast — *A Free Unsullied Land*
Darrell Kastin — *Shadowboxing with Bukowski*
Coleen Kearon — *Feminist on Fire*
Coleen Kearon — *#triggerwarning*
Jan English Leary — *Thicker Than Blood*
Diane Lefer — *Confessions of a Carnivore*
Rob Lenihan — *Born Speaking Lies*
Colin Mitchell — *Roadman*
Ilan Mochari — *Zinsky the Obscure*
Peter Nash — *Parsimony*
Peter Nash — *The Perfection of Things*
Gregory Papadoyiannis — *The Baby Jazz*
Pelham — *The Walking Poor*
Andy Potok — *My Father's Keeper*
Kathryn Roberts — *Companion Plants*
Robert Rosenberg — *Isles of the Blind*
Fred Russell — *Rafi's World*
Ron Savage — *Voyeur in Tangier*
David Schein — *The Adoption*
Lynn Sloan — *Principles of Navigation*
L.E. Smith — *The Consequence of Gesture*
L.E. Smith — *Travers' Inferno*
L.E. Smith — *Untimely RIPped*
Bob Sommer — *A Great Fullness*
Tom Walker — *A Day in the Life*
Susan V. Weiss — *My God, What Have We Done?*
Peter M. Wheelwright — *As It Is On Earth*
Suzie Wizowaty — *The Return of Jason Green*

Poetry
Anna Blackmer — *Hexagrams*
Antonello Borra — *Alfabestiario*
Antonello Borra — *AlphaBetaBestiaro*
Sue D. Burton — *Little Steel*
David Cavanagh — *Cycling in Plato's Cave*
James Connolly — *Picking Up the Bodies*

Greg Delanty — *Loosestrife*
Mason Drukman — *Drawing on Life*
J. C. Ellefson — *Foreign Tales of Exemplum and Woe*
Tina Escaja/Mark Eisner — *Caida Libre/Free Fall*
Anna Faktorovich — *Improvisational Arguments*
Barry Goldensohn — *Snake in the Spine, Wolf in the Heart*
Barry Goldensohn — *The Hundred Yard Dash Man*
Barry Goldensohn — *The Listener Aspires to the Condition of Music*
R. L. Green — *When You Remember Deir Yassin*
Gail Holst-Warhaft — *Lucky Country*
Raymond Luczak — *A Babble of Objects*
Kate Magill — *Roadworthy Creature, Roadworthy Craft*
Tony Magistrale — *Entanglements*
Andreas Nolte — *Mascha: The Poems of Mascha Kaléko*
Sherry Olson — *Four-Way Stop*
David Polk — *Drinking the River*
Aristea Papalexandrou/Philip Ramp — *Μας προσπερνά/It's Overtaking Us*
Janice Miller Potter — *Meanwell*
Philip Ramp — *The Melancholy of a Life as the Joy of Living It Slowly Chills*
Joseph D. Reich — *Connecting the Dots to Shangrila*
Joseph D. Reich — *The Hole That Runs Through Utopia*
Joseph D. Reich — *The Housing Market*
Joseph D. Reich — *The Derivation of Cowboys and Indians*
Kennet Rosen and Richard Wilson — *Gomorrah*
Fred Rosenblum — *Vietnumb*
David Schein — *My Murder and Other Local News*
Harold Schweizer — *Miriam's Book*
Scott T. Starbuck — *Industrial Oz*
Scott T. Starbuck — *Hawk on Wire*
Scott T. Starbuck — *Carbonfish Blues*
Seth Steinzor — *Among the Lost*
Seth Steinzor — *To Join the Lost*
Susan Thomas — *The Empty Notebook Interrogates Itself*
Susan Thomas — *In the Sadness Museum*
Paolo Valesio/Todd Portnowitz — *La Mezzanotte di Spoleto/Midnight in Spoleto*
Sharon Webster — *Everyone Lives Here*
Tony Whedon — *The Tres Riches Heures*
Tony Whedon — *The Falkland Quartet*
Claire Zoghb — *Dispatches from Everest*

Stories
Jay Boyer — *Flight*
Michael Cocchiarale — *Still Time*
Michael Cocchiarale — *Here Is Ware*
Neil Connelly — *In the Wake of Our Vows*
Catherine Zobal Dent — *Unfinished Stories of Girls*
Zdravka Evtimova —*Carts and Other Stories*
John Michael Flynn — *Off to the Next Wherever*
Derek Furr — *Semitones*
Derek Furr — *Suite for Three Voices*
Elizabeth Genovise — *Where There Are Two or More*
Andrei Guriuanu — *Body of Work*
Zeke Jarvis — *In A Family Way*
Arya Jenkins — *Blue Songs in an Open Key*
Jan English Leary — *Skating on the Vertical*
Marjorie Maddox — *What She Was Saying*
William Marquess — *Boom-shacka-lacka*
Gary Miller — *Museum of the Americas*
Jennifer Anne Moses — *Visiting Hours*
Martin Ott — *Interrogations*
Jack Pulaski — *Love's Labours*
Charles Rafferty — *Saturday Night at Magellan's*
Ron Savage — *What We Do For Love*
Fred Skolnik— *Americans and Other Stories*
Lynn Sloan — *This Far Is Not Far Enough*
L.E. Smith — *Views Cost Extra*
Caitlin Hamilton Summie — *To Lay To Rest Our Ghosts*
Susan Thomas — *Among Angelic Orders*
Tom Walker — *Signed Confessions*
Silas Dent Zobal — *The Inconvenience of the Wings*

Odd Birds
William Benton — *Eye Contact*
Micheal Breiner — *the way none of this happened*
J. C. Ellefson — *Under the Influence*
David Ross Gunn — *Cautionary Chronicles*
Andrei Guriuanu and Teknari — *The Darkest City*
Gail Holst-Warhaft — *The Fall of Athens*
Roger Leboitz — *A Guide to the Western Slopes and the Outlying Area*
dug Nap— *Artsy Fartsy*
Delia Bell Robinson — *A Shirtwaist Story*

Peter Schumann — *Bread & Sentences*
Peter Schumann — *Charlotte Salomon*
Peter Schumann — *Faust 3*
Peter Schumann — *Planet Kasper, Volumes One and Two*
Peter Schumann — *We*

Plays
Stephen Goldberg — *Screwed and Other Plays*
Michele Markarian — *Unborn Children of America*

Essays
Robert Sommer — *Losing Francis*

www.ingramcontent.com/pod-product-compliance
Lightning Source LLC
Chambersburg PA
CBHW052052110526
44591CB00013B/2174